To Angi

Best wishes

How To **STAND OUT**
In The Age of Advertising Overload

MIND CAPTURE

TONY RUBLESKI

Morgan James Publishing • NEW YORK

MIND CAPTURE

ISBN: 1-933596-65-1 (Paperback)

Published by:

MORGAN · JAMES
THE ENTREPRENEURIAL PUBLISHER ™
www.morganjamespublishing.com

Morgan James Publishing, LLC
1225 Franklin Ave Ste 32
Garden City, NY 11530-1693
Toll Free 800-485-4943
www.MorganJamesPublishing.com

Cover/Interior Design by:

Rachel Campbell
rcampbell77@cox.net

Habitat
for Humanity®
Peninsula
Building Partner

[advance reviews for MIND CAPTURE]

"This is an incredibly important book that gives you proven, practical ways to capture attention – the most valuable resource of all – and translate that attention into sales."

- Brian Tracy, President
Brian Tracy International

"Astonishing! Packed with ideas and strategies that work in the real world of business. Getting attention in a crowded market place is one of the major battles of the 21st century. Let this eye-opening street-smart book serve as your guide to increased profits and success - Guaranteed!"

- Joe Vitale, author
"There's A Customer Born Every Minute"

"*Mind Capture* offers great advice and is packed with powerful business-building tools. I highly recommend it."

- Ivan Misner, Ph.D
Co-Author of Master of Networking
Founder & CEO of BNI

"I Love it, it's great. A must for all in business, it's a treasure."

- Joe Girard, www.joegirad.com
Guinness Book of World's Records
"World's Greatest Salesman"

"The best - marketing for the 21st century – book I've read. *Mind Capture* is not about the noise, the clutter, the overkill and the come on. It's filled with facts and figures on what's needed, what's appropriate, and what's practical to generate new and repeat business in the age of advertising overload...Definitely a classic in its time."

- Raleigh Pinskey, author
"101 Ways To Promote Yourself"

"Great book from an experienced, proven and successful marketer. Reading *Mind Capture* it's easy to realize you're learning from a guy who's been there, done that... Be prepared to realize you might need to do some things differently if your business is to survive, and flourish!"

- Bob Burg, author
"Endless Referrals"
"Winning Without Intimidation"

"Any business sick of writing big checks to "hot" ad reps with little to show for it would do well to read Tony's book. *Mind Capture* demystifies marketing and has enough proven, profit producing strategies to keep you growing for a long time."

- Mike Attias, President
www.zrestaurantmarketing.com

"*Mind Capture* is a powerhouse of marketing ideas. Just implement one and watch your profits soar. If you have a phobia for marketing, Tony has the cure adding increased revenue to that all important bottom line."

- Jolene Aubel, President
Mountain Marketing and Communications

"Tony has made a slam-dunk, air-tight case for making marketing your number one business priority. Buy this book, apply what's inside and watch your sales explode!"

- Bob Negen. President
WhizBang! Training

"Tony's vast depth of knowledge and awesome use of humor have made this book a "must read"! *Mind Capture* is a road map for avoiding trial and error, and jumping straight to Success!"

- Dave Sheffield, President
Sheffield Enterprises

"Tony has captured the true essence of how marketing should be defined and utilized in the business world of the 21st century. I believe that *Mind Capture* provides thought-provoking proactive approaches that will lead to the ultimate success of any organization's marketing endeavors. A must read!"

- Greg Bauer, author
"The Breathing Blanket"

"Tony, you captured my mind with this book! *Mind Capture* truly lives up to its name. It's a potpourri of marketing wisdom, insights and real world applications. In this cluttered, rough sea of marketing messages, along comes the lifeboat - Mind Capture - to save business owners, entrepreneurs and marketers from the massive swells. Thanks for writing this masterpiece."

- Mike VanNorden
(*World's Foremost Publicity Expert*)
www.PublicityKing.com

"FINALLY...The TRUTH about marketing your business for RE-SULTS! Tony's *MindCapture* puts together ALL the basics you NEED to know to be successful in marketing your business in today's chaotic world of media and message overwhelm!"

- Alexandria Brown
"The Ezine Queen"
www.EzineQueen.com

"I know Tony Rubleski is the real deal after sharing the floor with him and getting to know him. When you learn to capture minds, you will automatically capture market share--and more importantly dollars! Listen, believe and incorporate everything this man has to say!"

- Glenn Dietzel, CEO
www.AwakenTheAuthorWithin.com

[dedication]

To Kim and my three little angels, Paige, Taylor and Braydon...your love, support and patience truly amaze me!

[table of contents]

SECTION I. THE MIND CAPTURE MINDSET

SECTION II. MIND CAPTURE MARKETING

SECTION III. MIND CAPTURE LOYALTY

[about the author]

Tony Rubleski is currently the president of Mind Capture Group, based in Spring Lake, Michigan. His duties include sales, expansion into new markets, copywriting, public relations and building Mind Capture! His work has been featured in Bottom Line Magazine, The Detroit Free Press and the Fox TV news network.

He possesses a degree in Marketing from Western Michigan University (1994) and has worked with a wide range of businesses ranging from casinos, insurance agents, banks, to restaurants, real estate agents and a wide range of entrepreneurs.

He was also selected as a contributing author for the recently released book *Walking With The Wise Entrepreneur* which also features Donald Trump, Bill Gates, Dr. Laura, Robert Kiyosaki, Dan Kennedy, Brian Tracy, and many other well known business personalities.

Schedule permitting, he's available for keynote and half-day speaking programs. He speaks to chambers of commerce, associations and sales teams on marketing and

I

sales strategies to stand out and win more business. His most popular programs include:

*Referral Magic: 27 Ways To Keep Customers Coming Back Again & Again
*Seven Secrets To Improve Your Marketing & Get More Sales
*How To Create Dynamic Marketing Materials That Build Mind Capture
*How To Get $100,000 In FREE Publicity
*Capturing The Mind of Your Customers

For more information:

Mind Capture Group
14864 Birchwood Dr.
Spring Lake, MI 49456

[II]

Phone: 616-638-3912
Fax: 616-842-2814
Email: tony@mindcapturegroup.com
Web: www.mindcapturegroup.com

[foreword]

Rip The Cover Off This Book!

There are books that have value even if never read. Such books' titles and cover concepts are so powerful that if all one did was frame the cover and put it on a frequently seen wall, it would serve well. 'Think And Grow Rich', 'Magic Of Thinking Big' come to mind. Tony has hit on such a book about marketing. After all, capturing the minds of prospects and clients is what we are all about. There's profit in the constant reminder that the job is, in fact, capture - not just communication. Not, God forbid, the ad agencies' assertion that you should invest in recognition. Not even just persuasion. No – *capture*.

A good question to ask yourself is: Are you capturing the minds of your customers?

Then, Tony has called this The Age Of Advertising Overload. He's not kidding. The proliferation and expansion of an overwhelming quantity of advertising clutter and a dizzying array of choices have made it monstrously challenging to wade through it, rise above it, and stand out from it, in order to gain favorable attention. Advertising Overload equals mass attention deficit disorder on consumers' part.

Media that briefly offer respite and clutter-free opportunity to its early adopters are quickly invaded and overwhelmed with clutter producers. The Internet is the most recent. Keeping forefront in your mind that you operate in an environment of Advertising Overload is useful.

In my own writings and seminars I teach, and in my consulting I frequently discover that entrepreneurs and marketers sabotage themselves solely by "underestimating the difficulty of the task." By that I mean many things. Having unrealistic expectations, tackling too big a market with too few resources, and presuming marketing messages will be paid attention purely because they are put forward.

Well, if Tony has accomplished all this with only the cover of his book, imagine how much value is contained in its pages!

I have known Tony for many years and admired his work. I hope he will not mind me taking some credit and mentioning that he has been a subscriber to my NO B.S. MARKETING LETTER, Member of my Inner Circle, and student of my methods for quite some time. You should pay attention to what he presents in MIND CAPTURE because, unlike so many authors, he is a street-wise, authentic practitioner. His book is the evolutionary result of his own legitimate, successful experience, making several businesses of his own work.

You can also feel good about having purchased this book as an act of profound charity and kindness. As you'll discover within its pages, Tony is a Detroit Lions fan. This is right up there with caring for lepers. It is a selfless act of suffering every fan of football must appreciate. It is fans like Tony who keep teams like the Lions in existence so our teams have opponents they can count on beating. Bless him.

Is there anything 'new' in this book? What's old to you is new to another and vice versa. But even if you are an exceptionally sophisticated, experienced marketer, Tony's book, at barest minimum, provides a well-organized, comprehensive review of every way you might marry smart direct-response marketing to virtually any product, service, business or professional practice. It is certainly good 'primer' to put into the hands of the employee, associate, friend, son or daughter you are trying to "bring up to speed" on the subject of smart marketing. With that in mind, you might want to order a bulk supply of these books. I mention that, well, because Tony told me to. (At the same time you might want to hand out copies of my book, 'The Ultimate Marketing Plan' too. I mention that because I own racehorses and they eat. A lot. I need the royalties).

Take the whole idea of MIND CAPTURE and run with it. Use this book as impetus to very deliberately strive to move beyond ordinary marketing, to a much greater and higher level of bonding with your clientele. Challenge yourself.

And seriously consider tearing the front cover off and sticking it up somewhere you'll see it often.

[VII]

Dan Kennedy
www.dankennedy.com

[introduction]

We live in an interesting age. Never before have people had so many choices, options, and marketing messages to choose from. As businesses compete to win new and repeat business, they're up against intense and nimble competition along with highly selective and skeptical prospects that've seen it all and believe little if any advertising they see.

This book will help you get into the wired, overloaded, headline- driven, and highly selective mind of today's busy prospect. We'll look at key challenges all marketers face and effective ways to blast through them. In addition, we'll look at the psychological traits and marketing tools needed by today's successful marketers if they intend to grow and prosper.

What is Mind Capture? This is not a simple one-word answer. In essence, think of Mind Capture as the valuable ability to get people's attention, awareness, and business through the use of superior marketing and follow-up skills.

Here's the amazing thing about the millions of dollars spent each day on marketing: Most of it's never seen, overly intrusive, annoying, offensive and flat out pathetic. Businesses of all shapes and sizes try to get cute or clever and then scratch their head's as to why the marketing function of the business isn't working. Marketing is looked at with disdain and often viewed as a necessary evil. This self-sabotaging behavior is the main reason most businesses are stuck in neutral year after year or have challenges trying to grow. Most refuse to see the importance of marketing or why they should work at getting better at it.

Why should you care about this thing called Mind Capture? Simple - Everything revolves around the ability to persuade and sell. Be it politics, education, parenting, religion, or business it all comes down to who can present the most compelling, believable and persuasive argument to win people's time, fleeting attention and trust. It may not seem fair, but it's the reality of the world we live in.

Everyone, regardless of societal status, is impacted and touched by the forces of marketing. There's no escaping or hiding from it. Marketing messages will always be present and continue to increase. With each new gadget or technology, comes a whole flood of new and skilled marketers ready to attack and grab your attention, with the hope of getting in your head and gaining Mind Capture.

SECTION 1 looks at key distinctions and fallacies most people have regarding today's competitive marketplace, and popular opinions related to marketing and customer service. It also examines why the proper marketing mindset is critical to achieving significant marketing breakthroughs.

SECTION 2 examines the weapons and tactics used to build successful marketing for any business. From positioning, vertical marketing, building evidence, and writing sales copy - to publicity and getting people's attention, this section serves as the fuel to increase sales and build Mind Capture.

SECTION 3 explores key elements to building loyalty with today's demanding and skeptical customer. In addition, we'll look at proven ways to get referrals from the best salespeople in any company – existing customers.

At the end of many sections you'll find additional resources listed that I consider extremely valuable for you to research and to build on the strategies you'll learn in this text. I've read hundreds of books, manuals, newsletters, and attended countless workshops and seminars the past 10 years in search of the pretenders versus contenders in the areas of marketing, advertising, sales, and public relations. If you explore even one-tenth of these you'll be ahead of 99% of the pretend "marketing experts" who couldn't sell or create an effective marketing piece if their life depended upon it.

I applaud and thank you for the investment of time and money to learn the secrets of *Mind Capture!*

OVER $170.00
in valuable FREE "Mind Capture" bonuses for you:

1.) CRITIQUE CERTIFICATE ($150.00 VALUE): Allows you the chance to fax or email any one specific marketing, pr or sales related question for personal review by author Tony Rubleski. (See next page and allow up to 3-4 weeks for response)

2.) FREE ISSUE OF TONY'S MONTHLY NEWS-LETTER "A CAPTURED MIND" ($20.00 VALUE): Send an email with subject line "Free newsletter issue - Mind Capture book offer" to info@mindcapturegroup.com. This newsletter is loaded with top marketing, sales, publicity, Internet, goal setting and motivation techniques and real world exhibits and ready to use marketing pieces. You also get a cd audio interview containing rare and valuable tips, and strategies from our special featured guest.

3.) FREE BI-WEEKLY ELETTER. Get "Captured" every two-weeks with fresh updates, strategies and marketing resources designed to help you by subscribing to the Mind Capture eletter. Simply visit www.mindcapturegroup.com and click on the eletter subscribe box on the home page.

[$150.00 critique certificate]

Entitles holder to submit any single letter; brochure; sales piece; advertisement; press release; or similar promotional material by mail for critique by author Tony Rubleski.

Name & Company _____

Address _____

City, State, Zip _____

Phone _____ Fax _____

E-Mail Address _____

Send Certificate and Materials To:
Mind Capture Group
14864 Birchwood Drive
Spring Lake, MI 49456

Terms & Conditions: Certificate expires 12 months from date of book purchase. Allow 3 to 4 weeks for Mr. Rubleski's response. Consult given by mail or email only. Actual finished materials or "rough draft" and copy for planned material may be submitted. Additional consulting may be contracted for, Mr. Rubleski's schedule permitting; fees quoted on request.

Please be advised that any materials submitted for review by Tony Rubleski, including those submitted with critique coupons may be published in any of Tony Rubleski authored/edited publications, as examples. Also, submitted materials will not be returned. Do not submit items you are concerned about keeping confidential. © 2006 Tony Rubleski.

CODE: USMC06

[who's Tony Rubleski and why should I listen to him?]

That's an excellent question to be asking before invest-
ing valuable time reading this book. Why? Because today
there are far too many false prophets teaching marketing
that have no business giving advice on the subject! Sadly, it's
a common tragedy that I see being repeated day after day
with businesses of all shapes and sizes.

*For example, I recently attended a workshop sponsored by
a large Chamber of Commerce titled* Marketing 101. *The in-
structor worked for a large accounting firm. Here's the problem folks: Her advice was based primarily on textbook theory
and she provided little, if any concrete success stories. Think
about this for a moment; a respected Chamber sponsors
her accounting firm to speak on the topic of marketing to its
membership. That's about as silly as me giving a seminar on
the new tax and accounting changes passed by Congress. Not
good, not credible and not honest!*

I'm not a household name (yet!) by any means but I think
it's important for you to know more about the sources, expe-
riences and real-life applications that have helped to shape
the skills and strategies contained in this book.

A QUICK <u>WARNING</u>:

This book is not based on tons of academic research. Not that I'm opposed to that (I do have a Marketing degree from a four-year college), but I feel it's vital to share with you information that works in the real world of business – not in the academic fantasy world. The goal of this book is to give you proven "firepower" that's been tested, refined and crafted to get results! In addition, at the end of many chapters, additional resources are listed for you to investigate and use for your business.

————————————

I'd like to give you a quick snapshot on where I've been and on what basis I created and wrote this book from. Here are 15 Things About Me That I Think You Should Know Before Reading *Mind Capture*:

1. I spent nine years in the highly competitive telecom industry selling door-to-door to residential and business customers. So I wouldn't starve and have to make cold-calls eight hours a day, I became a serious student of marketing and sales. I'm extremely thankful that I developed a love and passion for learning.

2. I have a degree in Marketing from a four-year university, but an MBA from the real world of business. Requirements for my MBA include being able to out-sell, out-market and out-think my competitors. Advanced marketing and effective sales skills are a powerful one-two punch that few people effectively use or are willing to learn to achieve magnificent breakthroughs.

3. I have three children (8, 6, 3) and a very patient wife (St. Kim) who inspires, teaches, motivates and provides wonderful insights to me each day. Many a great marketing idea has come to me while watching a Disney movie with my wife and kids.

4. An active member of Toastmaster's International for eleven years - One of the <u>best</u> organizations around for fine tuning someone's ability to communicate, sell, persuade and lead more effectively.

5. A few key mentors that I must thanks for their support, inspiration and teaching: Dan Kennedy, Jim Rohn, Greg Bauer, Michael Wickett, Maxwell Maltz, Robert Allen, Jeffrey Gitomer, Jack Canfield, Tony Robbins, Jay Abraham, Linda Delean (WMU), and one of the best unknown marketers around; my brother Jeff. In addition, I would like to thank the thousands of clients who've given me the opportunity to serve them for the past 12 years… I'm looking forward to many more great years!

6. I'm driven, determined and damn persistent. I truly believe that life is very short and we're here to live life to the fullest each day. There are NO time-outs in life and we can only learn from the past and strive to get better in the future.

7. I truly love helping others grow their businesses with effective marketing and advertising strategies. Be it through creating direct mail campaigns, new offers, marketing plans, or when I'm speaking to groups of business owners. I love being a part of marketing success stories.

8. My motto: Learn, earn and return each day. This may sound simple to most people but it drives me to keep growing my brain, business, and income, while at the same time giving back to fellow entrepreneurs and my community.

9. I firmly believe in giving back to others on a daily basis. Be it monetary or through volunteer efforts in the community. Thanks again for purchasing this book. A percentage of sales will be given back to Junior Achievement of the Great Lakes to help teach economics and free enterprise to students in K-12th grade.

10. I've been told I have "rushing sickness" by many. I'm always in a hurry trying to squeeze out as much as possible from each day because my dreams and goals inspire and drive my ambitions. My wife will attest that I hate being late for anything and that I'm continually amazed at how people squander and waste their precious time on petty problems.

11. I almost became a Catholic priest. I couldn't resist throwing in a strange bit of trivia in here somewhere. Yes, it almost happened but the big Man upstairs had other plans in mind for me.

12. I love looking at the psychology behind effective marketing and sales. Being curious and asking questions is an important skill to use for discovering why certain forms of promotions and advertising work better and out-perform others.

13. Marketing should always be the #1 priority in any business. You'll discover that I enjoy picking on accountants (they're not all bad by the way), because it always comes back to one key thing: no new or repeat business and you'll soon be out of business. If you're not in business the accountant loses too. In my opinion, most accountants treat marketing and sales with little respect because frankly they suck at it. They think selling is a dirty word. Because they don't understand marketing and sales does not give them the right to kill a business with bad advice.

14. I love small business. 97% of the companies in the U.S. employ fewer than 100 people. I'm not against the Fortune 500's of the world, but I am opposed to a lot of the methods they're utilizing to give the illusion that they're growing. It's very easy and popular these days to bash CEO's but let's face it; exorbitant executive pay and continual downsizing are defensive strategies which the economy and investors continue to pay for.

I'm very disappointed with many CEO's today who claim to be leading and growing their company with innovation, teamwork and increased sales. If you're making that kind of money as an executive, you'd better be damn good at marketing and not simply a mad butcher (AKA: "Chainsaw" Al Dunlap) who specializes in downsizing, rightsizing or whatever new and insulting term they come up with for putting people out of work.

The "wait and see" mentality running rampant in the economy today is pathetic. New, aggressive (often small business owners) and hungry competitors are working hard every day to grow and effectively market to get more business - not defend what they already have! The media would have you think that we should fold up the tents, close our businesses, hide in a cave and wait around for Alan Greenspan or the federal government to magically save and bail out the economy. Ridiculous!

15. Today I own Mind Capture Group based in Spring Lake, Michigan. I help organizations improve their marketing and sales programs ranging from direct mail, referral programs to publicity and attracting new customers. I frequently speak to business groups and sales teams on ways to build Mind Capture and increased profits.

───────────────

There you have it - 15 things about me that hopefully shed a little more light on my experience and opinions expressed throughout this book. I hope you find the strategies and techniques covered in this book important in growing your business. I wish you much success in your marketing efforts to build Mind Capture!

Keep me posted on your progress, I'd love to hear from you. My email address is tony@mindcapturegroup.com. I also recommend subscribe to my free bi-weekly eletter which is jam-packed with additional marketing, publicity, sales and promotion ideas. Visit: www.mindcapturegroup.com.

THE MIND CAPTURE MINDSET

[chapter 1]

"YOU WANT THE TRUTH. YOU CAN'T HANDLE THE TRUTH!"

Jack Nicholson
From the film: A Few Good Men

As we started the year 2006, I kept looking for a quote that would sum up my feelings as to why so many small and mid-sized businesses have taken it on the chin the past few years in the United States. Is it greed? Bad judgment? Fear? The economy? While these four reasons can't be overlooked I think the quote from Jack Nicholson (who plays a tough, direct marine in the movie *A Few Good Men)* sums up why many businesses are in dire straits. Like a deer frozen in the headlights of an oncoming automobile, their sales are paralyzed due to denial and a lack of marketing savvy.

When boom times were everywhere and the phone simply rang with new leads and business, most companies became extremely complacent and spoiled. No thought was given to creating a solid marketing plan that could weather good or bad economic conditions to generate new and repeat business. Now that the phone has stopped ringing,

3

and "old" ways of getting business aren't producing results, a real sense of panic has set in.

I'LL CUT TO THE CHASE AND REVEAL A SECRET ABOUT MARKETING THAT SIMPLY BAFFLES ME

When it comes to marketing most businesses have no clue. I could show them 50 proven ways to crank up their business during a consultation or seminar; look them in the eye; get a firm commitment they'd make positive changes and know almost for certain that many would keep doing the same old thing. They'd scream, kick and moan because their results didn't change because they didn't try anything new!

The scary part; give most companies a perfect marketing map on how to grow their business and they'd still find a way to screw it up. How do I know this to be true? I see it everyday with business owners and company presidents I meet with. While it's particularly true with most small businesses, I see it often in larger companies that have entire marketing teams or ad agencies at their disposal. The standard comment "we already have an agency" is a simple cop out and frankly a dangerous attitude to take regarding the lifeblood of any business – marketing!

I know some of you reading this are thinking, "this guy sounds like a drill sergeant from the Marine Corps" and that's good. There are too many pretend "experts" (often your own employees) out there collecting ad agency fees or a paycheck, giving poor marketing advice and then disappearing or making excuses when the painful results become clear.

THE DIRTY SECRET THAT MOST AD AGENCIES DON'T WANT YOU TO KNOW ABOUT!

I read about this many years ago in a special report published by marketing guru Dan Kennedy that simply shocked me. He broke down what most ad agency's think about when it comes

to serving clients. Now that I'm in the ad game full-time I can honestly tell you that he's pretty much right on target with the following summation:

AGENCY GOALS:

1. *Win awards*
2. *Be creative*
3. *NO accountability*
4. *Encourage client to spend more money*
5. *Client retention*
6. *Your return on investment*

YOUR GOALS:

1. *Get new business, leads*
2. *Return on investment*
3. *Accountability*

WHY DO MOST AD AGENCIES HATE DIRECT RESPONSE MARKETING?

It makes them have to produce and show results. There can be no excuses for poor performance. Creativity and "branding" are key terms agencies will throw out as selling points, but when it comes back to results they often promise little if anything because they know they can't. Excuse me, but that's not a good way to spend your money on marketing and sales.

The statement; "that's the way we've always done it" should be banned from every company, and the person uttering it, fired on the spot. The sad state of most struggling businesses or industries can be directly traced back to this ignorant way of thinking about competitors and taking bad advice from pretend marketing experts both inside and outside their organizations.

So where am I going with my ranting and raving to open up this book? Simple: By improving your marketing you can grow, stand out, and dominate your market! No matter what excuses others will come up with (economic conditions, prices, interest rates, the President, blah, blah, blah) you'll be bulletproof. Those who market best and build MIND CAPTURE in today's intense, 24/7 society will stand out head and shoulders above the rest.

you want the truth. you can't handle the truth!

Too Much Noise!

Let's face it; today's consumer is smarter, extremely demanding, and more cynical than ever. With the average barrage of over 1500 advertising messages thrown at them daily, they've built up excellent radar systems for detecting and screening out "uninvited" marketing messages.

So here's the magic question: How do companies market effectively to stand out and get new business? This is a difficult question to answer. In the old days, which sadly most businesses still think exist, you'd simply find a decent location, open your doors and wait for customers to drop in. I have to wake you from this foolish dream. This "retail" mentality puts at least 85% of the businesses in the marketplace out of business within three to five years.

It's still amazing to me how many businesses simply sit back and wait for customers to appear at the door. This is what I call "lazy marketing" because there's no real game plan for getting new business. In addition, once they actually get a customer, they commit the biggest sin of all: Making little if any attempt to offer them additional products or services on a regular and consistent basis.

Here's a quick suggestion to help your marketing efforts with existing customers: Be FUN to do business with. Continually be on the lookout for ways to delight and have fun with people through special events, communications, contests and announcements. Too many businesses are "transactional only" when dealing with existing customers. They act like robots showing little if any interest beyond performing a service, getting paid and moving onto the next thing.

Many firms have great products and services but no one knows they exist. If they treated marketing as a priority they would grow faster and often times leave their competition in the dust. The world is full of great products and services, but it always comes back to this key point:

"Superior marketing = superior growth"

[chapter 2]

MIND CAPTURE

What is MIND CAPTURE? Mind capture is simply the ability to stand out, get attention, and win new business in a world with too many choices and demands placed on people's time.

How do we get prospects to listen to our marketing messages? This is a difficult question but let me throw out an important clue.

Realize the external societal forces you're up against when creating marketing and advertising pieces

Here are *6 Key Characteristics of the 21st Century Customer* that you must acknowledge and consider to achieve maximum success.

1.) They're extremely cynical

2.) Too many choices

3.) Bombarded with 1500+ marketing messages a day

4.) Excellent at tuning out marketing messages

5.) Smarter than ever

6.) Time starved

Cynical. With the meltdown of trust in large corporations (Enron, WorldCom, etc.) and the romantic escapades of our former President and other elected officials, realize that people are extremely cynical. Everyday it seems a new scandal breaks, and those once held in high esteem have been taken down due to poor judgment and blatant acts of dishonesty.

This carries over to marketing as well. Because consumers have been left high and dry in the past or promised the world from a shady competitor, they're very reluctant to believe your marketing messages. You've got to prove that your company will back up its claims and also make them look good for choosing you.

Too many choices. Open a phone book and look up the section marked "attorney". Let me guess that there are multiple pages listing hundreds of lawyers in your city alone. In many industries the competition is fierce, and customers will naturally hold their suppliers to the fire due to the fact there's a long line of competitors outside the door begging for their business.

1500+ messages a day. This statistic ranges from 1000 to 3000 marketing messages bombarding people every day so we'll split the difference. Today's customer lives in the age of information overload. There's radio, TV, Internet, cell phones, newspapers, mail and email to name a few. Customers are saturated with an incredible amount of marketing messages. Everywhere you turn someone's trying to get your attention or what I call "mind capture".

This marketing noise will continue to grow as creative marketers look for any slight edge they can get to attract people's attention. I highly recommend you check out the film *Minority Report* with Tom Cruise if you want to see an interesting look at what futuristic marketing could look like if technology can keep up.

Excellent at tuning out marketing messages. With the massive amount of marketing noise, stimuli and messages being thrown at people each day, they've gotten very good at detecting and tuning out marketing messages. The challenge ALL marketers face is getting decision makers to take a few seconds to notice their message and present enough compelling reasons or curiosity for them to read your direct mail piece, email, fax, or listen to an ad or live sales rep.

The "BS detector" is always on!

Smarter than ever. With the age of information and the Internet it's easy for prospects to research hundreds of competing products, services, prices and references with the click of a mouse. The Internet may not be as glamorous and sexy as it was a few years ago, but realize that it's not going away. People will use it to shop, do research and look for ways to improve their life and business.

Time starved. People are busier than ever. They want convenience and things that will save time. Why do you think FedEx is so successful? They promise speed and peace of mind. If you can tailor your product or service to this way of thinking you're business will prosper.

In every marketing message or piece that we create for our own business or teach others how to do in workshops or one-on-one consulting, I continually mention that these six characteristics must not be overlooked. We're trying to get in the mind of the prospect and overcome certain barriers of resistance that we know our marketing message must address if we're going to achieve any degree of success.

Watch out for the wolf in sheep's clothing!

It seems these days everybody's in the advice game. "You should do this, you should do that". There's no shortage of so-called "experts", especially when it comes to giving marketing and advertising advice. Please be careful who you get and take

[11]

mind capture

advice from; and ask tough questions about the person or their company's background, expertise and documented results.

It simply boggles my mind when I meet with or call on companies that use CPA firms to handle their marketing. Now I'm not trying to discredit CPA's out there, but let me explain how dangerous this is. Realize that most accountants have no clue or real world training in marketing and sales. Heck, many of them are afraid of "sales types"; so why in the world would any Entrepreneur ask them for marketing advice? Think about that for a minute...that's INSANE!!!

Here's a simple thing to remember: *Business owners generate the money through sales and marketing - accountants keep track of it!* It's that easy. No complex formulas or theory, just proven advice that you should hold your accountant to.

The CPA who was also a "marketing genius"

Here's a true story about a CPA I dealt with in my area that proves my theory. The agency I was VP of at the time sent invitations out to different ad agencies and consultants inviting them to a free luncheon in order to demonstrate a new signage product we marketed. I get an email reply back from one of the firms we invited that went like this:

To: tony@captivate.com
Date: Tuesday, April 16 2005
Subject: upcoming seminar

Tony~

Just wanted to let you know that we would not be attending the seminar on May 9.

A bit of marketing advice: If you want to tout your firm as a wellspring of new ideas, perhaps you don't want to copy the advertising message for MasterCard on the record (invitation) you sent.

> John Smith, CPA
> Managing Director
> XYZ Marketing

Let me quickly evaluate and point out the valuable lessons learned from this email I received:

1.) **John (not his actual name) should never be hired to give marketing advice. He rips us for borrowing a very powerful ad campaign used by MasterCard. In marketing circles we call this CREATIVE THEFT! Why re-invent the wheel when there's already a successful promotion we can tweak (not outright copy) and use for our promotions.**

2.) **This mail piece pulled a 25% response rate. He read it and so did just about everybody else we sent it out to as well. I'll take a 25% response rate on a mailing anytime.**

3.) **Look at John's title "CPA & Managing Director". He's the head of marketing and a CPA for a major ad agency in our market. I've got a final piece of advice for John, Stick to being a CPA, not a so-called Marketing Manager.**

[13]

mind capture

[chapter 3]
TOO MANY PEOPLE STANDING AROUND TAKING UP SPACE

I have to thank my wife for the title of this chapter, because she summed up my innermost feelings and frustrations as to what holds far too many businesses hostage from achieving true success - bad advice, opinions, and poor judgment calls that stifle growth and take any element of innovation and fun out of the business.

Follow me here; this may be the most important point of the book. It may appear I'm deviating from marketing principles but it's critical to understand the overall impact incompetent employees, partners, lawyers and accountants have on most businesses.

If you own any kind of business always be thinking in the back of your mind: "Is this person creating positive solutions, generating new ideas and adding to the bottom line or are they just standing around taking up space?" This may sound harsh but never forget – in spite of guilt trips and roadblocks people will place in your way, you're the one taking the risk, making payroll and striving to grow a profitable enterprise.

How does this play into marketing? Many ways: As you implement changes recommended in this book within your company regarding more accountability, sales goals, customer retention and implementation of new marketing concepts you'll face intense resistance from many in and outside your organization. Count on it.

Your accountant might flip out because they think you're spending too much on retention programs, referrals, and marketing. Your employees often will not understand why you're trying to be different and doing "unconventional" things they've never seen. Your lawyer will question your motives when you promote powerful guarantees and testimonials in your marketing. Again, count on massive resistance. It WILL appear.

The businesses that outshine the competition treat marketing and innovation as their #1 priorities. Competitors will often be the biggest critics of their aggressive and sometimes controversial marketing tactics because they're jealous and they work. The system of free-enterprise rewards risk takers and those that deliver superior value.

If you've got the competition complaining about your marketing you're onto something. Keep doing what you're doing. In spite of massive resistance from many people the temptation will be to stop what's working and play it safe. Playing it safe mentality is for those who should be employees not entrepreneurs!

Far too many people in the media, unhappy employees (sadly a majority at most companies) and tenured academic type, will be glad to support and backup what former Disney marketing guru Mike Vance calls "pissers and moaners" thinking when it comes to growing a business in challenging economic times. That's a great parallel description for negative behavior and the taking up space mentality that is running rampant in today's business climate.

Never forget there's no such thing as "friendly" competition. This is a huge lie taught in far too many business schools by instructors with little, if any, real world experience. Get your advice from seasoned, battle-tested veterans who've got the experience and large bank balances to back up their claims. If someone starts to spout off advice ask yourself the magic question: "Is this person really trying to help my business grow or are they simply taking up space?"

It's Real Simple:

Get Busy

Get Moving

Quit Your Complaining

Tune out "Pissers & Moaners"

Outfox and Outhussle Your Competition

[chapter 4]

"IF YOU BUILD IT. THEY WILL COME."

This saying was made famous in the classic film, **Field Of Dreams**, which starred Kevin Costner. Here's the ironic part: Most businesses believe that if they simply pick out a good location or have a decent product or service, customers will magically appear and do business with them.

WAKE UP FOLKS! THIS IS ABOUT AS FOOLISH AS A GROWN ADULT WALKING AROUND SAYING THEY STILL BELIEVE IN THE TOOTH FAIRY!

This is what I call the *Field of Dreams Syndrome*. Companies of all shapes and sizes usually acquire this deadly syndrome after a period of time when their business is established and running and overconfidence has set in. Simple ways to identify it within a business when you talk with upper management or owners include:

"We don't need to spend money on marketing or advertising"

"We get all of our business from referrals so we're going to cut back on our marketing"

"We've got a great location here, so we know people will stop in"

"Oh, we tried that form of advertising (direct mail, display ads, etc.) and it didn't work for us"

"We're not exactly sure where our new customers are coming to us from"

We've all heard these statements and I honestly think a lot of them are BS. More often than not you'll hear these kinds of comments from established businesses that have achieved some degree of growth or success initially.

Here's the problem with this line of thinking. Too many businesses are not pro-active with their marketing or even have a written plan set down on paper. If the economy changes, a major client drops them, new competitors appear, or any other forces out of their control occur, the business faces serious problems due to a lack of planning and laziness.

THE SECRET BEHIND SUCCESSFUL BUSINESS AND HOW THEY AVOID THE "FIELD OF DREAMS SYNDROME"

Here's the simple answer: They treat marketing and advertising as the #1 priority in their business!

They create and use a strong marketing mix to insure growth, and to provide a stream of new prospects that are willing and able to do business with them. It's that simple folks. The next few chapters we'll look at proven and effective ways for building and using a marketing mix for your business.

KEY CONCEPT: *The Field of Dreams Syndrome.* **Foolish belief that customers will magically appear with little if any effort.**

MIND CAPTURE LESSON: Always stay pro-active with your marketing efforts. Create and use a marketing plan.

ACTION: If you don't have a written sales and marketing

plan that you're using, reviewing and updating - get busy. How can you get to your destination without accurate instructions? This is the critical foundation piece.

Additional Mind Capture Resources:

Book: *"Getting Everything You Can Out of All You've Got"*
    by Jay Abraham
Book: *"The Ultimate Marketing Plan"* by Dan Kennedy
Book: *"Winning Through Intimidation"* by Robert Ringer

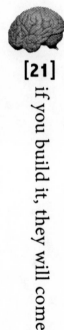

if you build it, they will come

[chapter 5]
GOD'S NEW VOICEMAIL SYSTEM

eadline:
"In Major Restructuring Move God Forced
To Eliminate 10,000 Angels and Install
New Voice Mail System In 2006!"

From: God
To: Citizens of the Earth
Date: December 31, 2005

Subject: Voice Mail

Most of you have learned to live with "voice mail" as a
necessary part of being on Earth. Because of the increased
amount of requests, complaints, and slow response times,
I've decided to install voice mail.

To improve our service and pay for the new system, we've
unfortunately been forced to lay off 10,000 angels who I'm
sure you can use at the present time on earth. St. Peter, my

CAO (Chief Angelic Officer) made it very clear that these angels were part of a major restructuring move. With the challenging economy, we're simply overburdened with additional prayers and requests at this time - thus the need for voice mail.

When you pray from now on, you'll hear one of the following options:

Press 1 for Requests

Press 2 for Thanksgiving

Press 3 for Complaints

Press 4 for all others

I'm sorry; all of our angels and saints are busy helping other sinners right now. However, your prayer is important to us and we will answer it in the order it was received. Please stay on the line.

If you would like to speak to:

Me (God), Press 1

For Jesus, Press 2

For the Holy Spirit, Press 3

To find a loved one that has been assigned to Heaven, Press 4, then enter his or her social security number, followed by the pound key.

If you receive a negative response, please hang up and try area code 666.

Our computers show that you have already prayed today. Please hang up and try again tomorrow. The office is now closed for the weekend to observe a religious holiday.

If you are calling after hours and need emergency assistance, please contact your local pastor.

IS THE PERSON ANSWERING YOUR TELEPHONE SLOWING KILLING YOUR BUSINESS?

It's amazing how many businesses put the most incompetent or rude person in charge of answering the phone. We've all had our own personal horror stories so there's no need to elaborate in great detail, but let me throw out a simple customer service idea that ties in perfectly with marketing.

Treat incoming calls like gold. If handled well, you make money. If they're not (which is often the case) your company is guilty of the following:

1.) **Ticking off existing clients who might never come back if treated poorly**

2.) **Wasting time, energy, and marketing dollars by placing the wrong person in charge of handling leads and inquiries**

3.) **Presenting a negative and incongruent message about your business, people, products and services**

4.) **Inability to track where leads, referrals, and possible complaints are coming from**

OK TONY, HOW DOES THIS RELATE TO MARKETING?

Simple: Treat your telephone system or switchboard operator like gold. First impressions are critically important because you'll often not get a second chance. If you're rolling out a new mailing, promotion or offer make sure the phone lines are beefed up to handle leads and new orders.

CASE IN POINT: The telephone and cable companies. They preach "excellent customer service" but the first time you call them you spend 15 minutes on hold waiting for

God's new voicemail system

someone in a different state to come on the line and give you the run around.

It's sad today how many people fight to win your business but as soon as you call them for anything they completely drop the ball. This is a bad, bad marketing strategy.

The second key thing to be on the lookout for is accountability with telephone leads. Make sure you're tracking the call in dates. Assign responsibility with follow up dates and reports to determine how leads are being handled. Did the person get the information they requested? Did they speak with someone in sales? If not, why?

Too many businesses spend a ton of money to generate leads but have inadequate systems in place to effectively deal with them. Time is money. The speed of response and first impression are the top two priorities when dealing with customers, leads, questions and referrals!

KEY CONCEPT: *Treat incoming calls like gold.* Employ a competent, well-trained person to take incoming calls or use a simple, hassle-free (a few prompts – not 100) voicemail system for your business.

MIND CAPTURE LESSON: Too many businesses make the critical mistake of mishandling calls and it ends up costing them a fortune.

ACTION: Evaluate who currently answers your company telephone and get feedback from customers on ways to make it easier to do business with you. If you find problems in your business here are a couple of solutions: 1. Get the person in training or fire them 2. Seek out a reliable call service or voicemail package.

Additional Mind Capture Resources:
Call Centers: ProPhone Communications at 1-231-733-1212
Book: *"Phone Power"* by George Walther

[section 2]

MIND
CAPTURE
MARKETING

[chapter 6]

OFFENSE VS. DEFENSE

When I was in the telephone business selling local and long-distance phone services – which by the way is probably the most hated industry on the planet – we had a seasoned, battle-tested director of sales who used to drill us on what he called "being offense minded versus defense minded".

What did he mean? Simple: make sure you're doing more "offense" related activities each day to generate enough prospects and leads in the sales funnel to hit and exceed your monthly sales quotas.

He cautioned us about not getting caught up and distracted by the daily "defense activities" such as maintenance, paperwork, wasted meetings, etc. that seemed to consume so many unsuccessful sales reps.

This same analogy relates to your marketing. How much time are you spending each day to promote, generate new leads, meet with serious prospects and create new business? My guess - not nearly as much time as you could or should be!

Yeah, I know you're busy running the show, training new staff, checking emails, sitting in meetings, and doing a host of other activities that are quite honestly good excuses for pushing marketing and promotions to the back burner. Please **realize that** most daily activities are chewing up valuable "offense" time and are purely **defense-minded**.

People get blinded each day doing busy work and before they can stop and look at the clock it's 5:15 PM and they haven't done anything in the offense category to insure future leads and deal flow.

The #1 reason this happens: Most business owners let others dictate their day with little if any resistance. So what's the secret to generating more "offense" in my opinion?

The <u>POWER</u> of Consistent, Clearly Defined Weekly, Monthly, Quarterly and Yearly Marketing Goals

You've all been through goal setting 101 but I wonder if amnesia has set in for most business owners. If you ask them to show you their sales and marketing goals, many of them; either A.) go into denial and excuse mode; or B.) throw out a ballpark number they "hope" to achieve.

I shockingly see this type of thinking with most businesses and it's downright dangerous. I'm a firm believer in having clearly defined marketing goals. Here are a few suggestions:

1.) Write down your plan for generating new business and stick to it. If it's in your head and not on paper you lose a lot of impact. There's something magical about putting things down on paper. This crystallization of thoughts and dreams to pen and paper is critical to achieving massive success.

2.) Assign timelines for marketing projects complete with due dates for implementation. If you don't put a deadline on getting things done, you'll end up extremely frustrated when you have too many irons in the fire and little if anything to show for it. Weekly, monthly, quarterly and yearly goals should all be used to push performance and insure that you're tracking and seeing positive results with your sales and marketing.

3.) Take 15 – 20 minutes before the workday begins to review today's schedule and check it against your written goals. This is critically important to goal setting but often the hardest step for people to pull off. Making this a priority and a habit in your daily life is extremely important if you want to make the breakthroughs you desire in your business or any other facet of your life.

4.) Block out time away from the office for planning, finishing key projects, brainstorming, and reviewing your progress. Set up scheduled appointments with yourself to reflect, measure your progress, set new goals and celebrate success-fully completed projects. Time spent on thinking and plan-ning will save you a great deal of time and make you even more productive.

├─────────────────┤

Later in the book we'll explore key marketing questions you should be asking to help you set, create and build powerful mar-keting goals in your business.

This seems like common sense but based on the large number of businesses that go out-of-business each year, I bet that few if any had written goals.

Goals are Dreams with a deadline!

├─────────────────┤

KEY CONCEPT: *Offense versus Defense.* Trap of getting caught up in unimportant tasks versus focusing on revenue pro-ducing activities.

MIND CAPTURE LESSON: Written sales and marketing goals that are continually reviewed, updated and put into action are critical to success in business.

ACTION: Look at the current state of your business. Are you trapped in "defense" activities? Review and update your sales and marketing goals on a consistent basis. Structure your day with "offense" minded activities to make them a reality!

Additional Mind Capture Resources:

Book: *Eat That Frog* by Brian Tracy

Book: *No B.S. Time Management* by Dan Kennedy

Book: *Awaken The Giant Within* by Anthony Robbins

Book: *7 Strategies for Wealth & Happiness* by Jim Rohn

Audio: *It's All Within Your Reach* by Mike Wickett (contact Nightingale Conant at 800-323-5552)

Audio: *Dreams Don't Have Deadlines* by Mark Victor Hansen (Nightingale Conant)

Book: *The Success Principles* by Jack Canfield

Book: *Secrets To Creating Wealth* by Stephen Pierce

Professional organizer: Mary Elward at 616-453-2976

[chapter 7]

VOICEMAIL MAGIC

What I'm about to share in this next chapter could have a massive, life-changing impact on your sales and communications if applied. Having spent over a decade successfully selling to hard to reach decision makers via the telephone I can tell you the strategies discussed here do work and will save you time, frustration and produce more sales.

Are you continually challenged by what I call "voicemail hell"? If you're like most people I consult, train and speak with at my workshops and trainings you answered "yes"!

If I could find the way to get every phone call and voice mail message returned I'd be a very, very rich man. While that's simply impossible, I would like to discuss a few techniques that WILL greatly increase your odds and the number of call backs you receive.

While designed to make life easier and make us more productive, all of us in sales and marketing know how truly frustrating voice mail can be in the communication process and in particular helping us to grow new sales. Buckle in, bring an open mind and let's begin.

Here are **three voice mail techniques** designed to help you get more phone calls returned:

#1. *The idea message.* We all as humans are always looking for new ideas to improve our lives, save time, make more money and help others. This is pure human nature at work. To tap into this as it relates to messages I highly recommend you become an "idea champion" when leaving messages for people.

Here's a quick example. Say you market health insurance to small business owners. You're calling on a small floral shop owner. You get the standard "Fred's not available, would you like to leave a voicemail?" You say yes and proceed. Here are a couple example messages you can adapt and modify to increase the odds of a return call.

> *"Hi Fred. This is Tony Rubleski at 616…. I'm located right here in town and had a couple of ideas I wanted to share with you and your team regarding the number one headache most local businesses have and a couple of new ways to solve it. I promise, only a couple of minutes, because I know you're incredibly busy. I'll be here for the next two hours at 616…"*

> *"Hi Jane. This is Tony Rubleski at 616…calling. I have a quick idea that I wanted to run by you that could make you and your entire staff quite happy. I'm not kidding. Many other local businesses were amazed after we discussed a couple of new options to improve their business. I'll be available until 10:30 AM at 616…"*

Why do this voice mail technique stand out and build **MIND CAPTURE**? Simple. Curiosity makes us think, wonder, and ask questions in our mind. New ideas spark our brain and our imagination. In addition, we're not revealing excessive amounts of information so a person can make a snap, impulse decision based on a voice mail message.

You'll also note that I put my phone number at the front of the call, mentioned the local connection, and that I would only need a couple of minutes. This makes it easier and less threatening for the person to call me back.

Please note: I'm not advocating deception here. You're goal is to get a return call and quickly share the idea(s) to determine if there might be a reason to discuss your product or service in greater detail.

#2. The "quick question" message. I can vividly remember a few years ago when I'd just gotten off the phone after leaving a voice mail and a fellow colleague looked at me with a huge grin and asked, "let me guess, you've got a quick question to ask?" I laughed out loud because he picked up and pointed out to me one of my favorite voice mail techniques for getting phone calls returned.

Here's a quick example scenario. Let's say you're marketing advertising services to local restaurant owners. The prospect you're calling is a pizza shop. You're calling one hour before they open and you're prompted to leave a message. Here are a couple messages you can leave to greatly increase the odds of a quick return call.

"Hi Mike. This is Tony Rubleski at 638…I'm calling from Spring Lake and had a quick question about one of the recent coupons you sent me. If you could give me a call back at 638…when you open this morning, I'd greatly appreciate it. Thanks!"

"Hi Sue. This is Tony Rubleski at 638…I had a quick question regarding your billboard on US-10 that I hoped you could answer for me. I'll be in until 11:30 AM. Thanks!"

Why does the quick question voice mail strategy produce **MIND CAPTURE?** Here are a few reasons:

1. It builds curiosity

2. It suggests that we need help to get a question answered

3. It doesn't imply a big time commitment on the prospects part

4. It offers a great segway (assuming you've HONESTLY explained why you had the question) to discuss what you provide that can possibly help their business

Again, make sure you leave your phone number at the beginning of the call and speak s-l-o-w-l-y so they can easily write down your information and not skip ahead because they can't decipher or hear what you're saying.

#3. *The name drop message.* This technique is sometimes frowned on by some people because they either don't understand how to do it properly or they fear the prospect will be offended when they mention a possible competitor in their industry.

Here's a quick example to study, modify for your business and implement immediately to help you get more messages returned. In this scenario you're selling radio advertising to a defined niche of auto dealership prospects. The gatekeeper or assistant upon receiving your phone call instantly asks, *"What's this regarding?"* At this point you can either get into a verbal boxing match if you goof up and aren't prepared to answer a question or you can ask to leave Joe Bigwig a voicemail.

"Hi Joe. This is Tony Rubleski in Grand Rapids at 638...I've helped a number of other dealerships in the region such as ABC Motors, GR Imports, and Best Buy Autorama to increase traffic at their locations and communicate more effectively with existing customers. I had a quick question regarding a recent ad I heard on WOOX. I'll be available until 10:30 AM at 638...Thanks!"

Why does this third voicemail technique build MIND CAPTURE?

1. It uses the power of association

2. It ignites one of the most powerful psychological triggers in marketing – fear of loss

3. It ties in a "quick question" which we discussed in the second voicemail technique

There you have it. Three powerful voicemail strategies to help you get more phone calls returned. Do the math. If you get just five more voicemail messages returned per week over an average of 50 weeks that's 250 additional opportunities. If you convert just 10% of these prospects that's an additional 25 new sales per year.

———————————————

KEY CONCEPT: VOICEMAIL MAGIC. Understanding how important it is to view the telephone and voicemail as a marketing weapon, not a roadblock.

MIND CAPTURE LESSON: By getting better at leaving powerful, attention getting voicemail messages you'll get more calls returned quicker and with better results.

ACTION: Review, modify and implement these three techniques within your business and reap the many benefits to your bottom line via increased time savings and new business.

Additional Mind Capture Resources:
Book: *Secrets of Question Based Selling* by Thomas Freese
Book: *You Can't Teach A Kid How To Ride A Bike At A Seminar* by David Sandler
Book: *The Little Red Book of Selling* by Jeffrey Gitomer

[chapter 8]

REACH OUT
AND GRAB SOMEONE!

In today's fast paced competitive world you must continually be on the lookout for ways to differentiate your marketing and promotions for maximum effectiveness.

One of the most powerful ways to pump up any sales letter, direct mail package, or follow packet to a qualified lead is via the use of "grabbers". Grabbers are simply objects you attach or include with a sales letter or information packet designed to help your information get noticed by today's super busy and easily distracted prospect.

The three main reasons for using them in your marketing:

1.) **To stand out and gain attention** from all the other mail, faxes, emails and communications that cross your prospect's desk.

2.) **To help differentiate** you from the competition. They help tie into the opening of your letter or information packet as to what products or services you provide.

3.) People remember them. As time starved as people are today you must be thinking "outside-the-box" to get your information looked at or even noticed.

20 Examples of Attention Grabbers And How To Use Them

#1. Coin Grabber. "Dear Joe: As you can see, I've attached a coin to the top of this letter. Why did I do this? Two reasons. First, to attract your attention to this letter. Secondly, because what I'd like to share with you concerns how you can make more money (save money) for your business by using XYZ..."

#2. Dice Grabber. "Don't Gamble with your next (mortgage, realtor, auto purchase)..."

#3. Playing Card (Ex. King/Queen card). "We treat our customers like royalty. Here are 5 reasons you should use ABC rentals for your next..."

#4. Red Envelope. This can be used to grab someone's attention because it's not your typical boring, white business envelope. Hand address the outside of the envelope and use a live stamp (avoid meter mail postage) for maximum effectiveness.

#5. Cassette or video. If you have client testimonials or video of your services in action, use this when following up with qualified prospects. A good video sent out with your printed information is a powerful 1, 2 combination.

#6. Plastic handcuffs. "Have you been handcuffed in the past by poor service, or lack of choices? We can help..."

#7. Shredded money. "Tired of spending money on office supplies that seem to cost a small fortune? At Tony's Office Products we can..."

#8. _Lottery ticket._ "We can increase the odds of success that you'll save money on your next dry cleaning bill. Thanks in advance for taking a minute to review our services. We hope you're a Winner in more ways than one!"

#9. _Plastic magnifying glass._ "Here are 5 reasons you should take a closer look at how XYZ Services can help you..."

#10. _Donuts._ Sounds crazy, but many businesses deliver boxes of donuts as an additional thank you to secretaries when dropping off sales/marketing information in person to key decision makers.

#11. _Puzzle Piece._ "Puzzled by the results you're getting from your current cell phone service? It doesn't have to be that way! Call Telephone Central to learn how you can..."

#12. _Clock or watch._ "Put us to the test! We ___ (clean, respond, act) faster than anyone in the market and ..."

#13. _Mock check or coupon._ "The check attached is not redeemable at any local bank, however it could be the most valuable bonus you've received in quite a while. It entitles you to (1/2 off, 1 free hour, etc.) consultation to discuss..."

#14. _Match stick._ "Dear John: As you can see I've attached a match to the top of this letter. Why? Two reasons: First, to get your attention; Secondly, because I have a burning, hot IDEA on how we can help you with..."

#15. _Aspirin packet._ "Dear John: Are your current taxes and payroll functions giving you a headache? We can help by..."

#16. _Band-Aid._ "Dear Sally: Are you tired of band-aid solutions to your current ____ (inventory, shipping, invoicing) needs? We can help by..."

[45]

reach out and grab someone

#17. Photograph. "As you can see I've attached a photo from a recent client we helped. Can we do the same for you? I'm confident we can…"

#18. Dollar bill. "Yes, that's a real dollar bill. I know you're busy so I wanted to reward you for taking a minute to review how ___ services can help you save time and money with your future/current ____ needs."

#19. Booklet or report. "Dear Mike: I know your firm does a lot of hiring and interviewing. I hope you find the enclosed special report, 5 Common Mistakes Employers Make When Hiring New Candidates, helpful. This report is based on our 15+ years of expertise in this area and…"

#20. Testimonial headline. "Dear Sue: The testimonial at the top of this letter is from a satisfied client who we recently helped…I'm confident we can help you do the same!"

KEY CONCEPT: *Reach out and GRAB someone!* People are time-starved and buried with communication. Use "grabbers" to make your marketing stand out from the competition.

MIND CAPTURE LESSON: The use of grabbers is critical to help you differentiate your marketing message from the sea of competing offers. Busy prospects and key decision-makers are inundated with tons of sales pitches and offers. A well thought out and executed grabber will increase your odds of getting noticed and being remembered.

ACTION: Use the 20-grabber ideas listed above to give you ideas. These are all quite cost effective and easy to implement into your current marketing.

[chapter 9]

THREE PROVEN WAYS TO DRIVE YOUR COMPETITION CRAZY!

The next few paragraphs are quite revealing, maybe even offensive to some of you, but I think they'll demonstrate a valuable marketing lesson.

In my mind there's no such thing as "friendly competition". Every day we're competing on the field of battle in search of new business, and either I'm getting the deal or my competition is. When I lose a deal it affects everyone in our company, including their families and mine.

If you have an excellent product or service, you should hate to lose. By missing the chance to work with a new client I've let them down and my company. Maybe this sounds harsh but I really believe it to be true.

In the marketing business I'm up against hundreds of media sales reps (newspaper, radio, TV, etc.), consultants and ad agencies who are trying to snipe marketing dollars away from my clients. This is a cold, hard fact of life and I know the competition is fierce. They could often care

49

less about the initiatives I'm trying to implement, and with this knowledge in mind here are a few ways to neutralize and keep them guessing.

Here are 3 ways to drive your competition crazy:

1.) Create and use a continuity program

2.) Continually roll out new offers and promotions

3.) Be fun to do business with

1. Continuity program. I call this "crack cocaine" marketing. What do I mean by such a strong comparison of this principle to cocaine you might be thinking? Simple: If you engineer your business with an effective way to keep your customers coming back again and again many of them will get hooked - similar to a drug-addict, who needs more and more.

Obviously, this is done in a way to help your customers and keep more of their dollars with you and not the competition. If you've broken through their initial barriers of skepticism and established that you provide a valued product/service, then you should seek out as many ways possible to do business with them.

To prove how true this is and how addicted I am to simple continuity programs, I opened my wallet during a recent workshop I was leading and counted 7 different programs that I use on a consistent basis. They included Subway, Heavenly Ham, GM Credit Card, Coffee Grounds, Great Harvest Bread, Pizza & Sub Shop and a local discount card I received in the mail.

I don't care what type of business you're in, there are a million ways to create continuity programs for your business that rewards loyal customers and keeps competitors away.

2. Continually roll out new offers and promotions.
I know this one seems like common sense, but I rarely see it done effectively if at all. By marketing more offerings that save your

customers' time and money and fulfill a need the better off everyone will be. Customers will appreciate it, you'll make more money and it will drive your competition nuts.

For example, in our company this year we've come out with two new service offerings - and continue to test and re-work our core business to increase sales, retention rates and better serve our customers. In 2007, we plan to introduce a minimum of two to three value added services for new and existing clients.

Through the effective use of promotions, testing, and providing new products/services, you'll blaze a trail in your industry that few if any competitors will be able to match or keep up with.

3. *Be fun to do business with.* It's amazing how many businesses are operated like faceless, nameless entities with no soul or personality. God knows we need more humor in the world - especially in the marketplace. You might be saying "our customers are too sophisticated" or "they'll be offended". Ridiculous. - that's a cop out!

Here are a few simple and effective ways to have fun with your customers:

1. *Mail creative and fun greeting cards throughout the year.* Look at your calendar and pick out which ones you could have fun with. For example, our company's Thanksgiving cards are the talk of the business community each year because we have fun with the season and our customers love it.

2. *Have contests involving cool prizes, discounts or popular TV shows and movies.* You could have a field day with this one. Almost every time we've rolled out a fun contest the payback has been huge in new business, referrals and positive feedback it's generated.

3. Send your customers' birthday, anniversary and congratulations cards. Come up with creative and clever ways of using cards to delight and surprise your customers. Example - a valued client has been with you for two years now. Send them a birthday card thanking them for two great years.

4. Hold client appreciation lunches or dinners for your top customers. This is a great way to have fun and strengthen relationships with your top customers. Bring in a guest speaker(s) and use it as a way to highlight their business, discuss your goals, and recognize how much you value doing business with them.

KEY CONCEPT: *Friendly competition is lie. Seek out ways to drive your competition crazy.* Keep your competition guessing, your customers happy and your bank balance growing.

MIND CAPTURE LESSON: By focusing on ways to better serve your customers through the use of continuity programs and being fun to do business with you'll clearly stand out in the market and leave your competition in the dust.

ACTION: This section gives you three ways to keep your competition guessing. Which method (s) will you implement immediately into your business? The choice is yours. Differentiate or risk becoming another boring, "average" business in your industry.

Additional Mind Capture Resources:

Book: *Start Small Finish Big* by Fred DeLuca
Book: *MindcontrolMarketing.com* by Mark Joyner
Book: *How to Drive Your Competition Crazy* by Guy Kawasaki
Book: *How to Get Customers to Call, Buy & Beg For More*
     by Ken Varga

[chapter 10]

15 WAYS TO INCREASE THE EFFECTIVENESS OF YOUR DIRECT MAIL, FAXES, POSTCARD AND EMAIL OFFERS

Most people are not professional copywriters. As a matter of fact they despise writing copy, but they still foolishly attempt to pull it off with little if any direction or training. Instead of looking for successful marketing efforts they can learn from, adapt and use in their business, they attempt to recreate the wheel.

With the flood of knowledge available on the topic of direct response I'd like to boil it down to a few concrete action steps you can use to bump up response rates in your direct marketing and make more money for your business.

Here are 15 easy ways to pump up your direct marketing efforts.

1. Use a headline. This is an ad for your ad. If your marketing piece doesn't have a good headline it's dead! Look at some of the top selling magazines such as Reader's Digest,

People Magazine, The National Enquirer or Good Housekeeping. What screams off their covers and makes you want to read more? The powerful, provocative and attention getting headlines.

2. Make it easy to contact you. Use multiple contact and response methods in all of your marketing communications. Use an 800#, fax number, email address and mailing address. Some people prefer one method versus another. You don't want to risk losing sales because of this simple yet often overlooked step.

3. Offer bonuses. A strong bonus offer attached to a specific deadline has been proven time and time again to help increase sales. They entice, motivate and reward the prospect or customer for taking immediate action. People by nature are very lazy. A well thought out bonus helps increase the chance they'll take action and respond to your offer.

4. Use guarantees. If you have an excellent product or service, back it up with a powerful, bold guarantee. The best way to find an effective one for your product/service is to look at what your competition isn't or will not guarantee that's a common problem, fear or inconvenience.

5. Use a complete order form. Make your order forms easy to understand and use. You'd be amazed at how difficult and confusing a lot of order forms can be. People are busy and have lots of choices. If it's difficult or an inconvenience to understand your order form, they'll usually stack them in the closest pile on their desk (to be thrown out later) or they'll simply buy from someone else.

6. Offer something for FREE. People love a good deal, especially something free. You could offer a free coupon, discount, sample, special report, video, or gift. Give them an irresistible reason to take action. In a lot of cases, they'll become a paying customer after you've lured them in by offering something of value for free.

7. *Create urgency.* Reward customers and prospects for taking immediate action or acting by a specific date. For example, you could offer early bird pricing or discounts based on specific dates or days of the week. With tons of competition in the marketplace you need to create as many reasons as possible to get people to take action.

8. *Make your message clear.* Don't be cute, or ramble on endlessly about product features. If the marketing piece isn't "you" driven with lots of benefits for the reader they won't respond. They're too busy to try and figure out why you want their attention, and they won't waste precious time on poorly written marketing pieces.

9. *Test, test, test.* Look for ways to fine-tune your marketing pieces through testing. It could be simply testing one headline versus another or the look of the outside envelope. Never stay content. Once you hit on a piece that's working, there's always the temptation to revamp it and make it better. Do simple tests such as a new headline, or different offer to get an accurate picture of why the changes performed or didn't perform better versus your control piece.

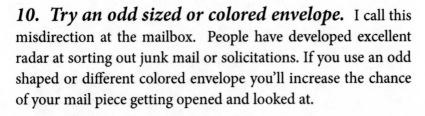

15 ways

10. *Try an odd sized or colored envelope.* I call this misdirection at the mailbox. People have developed excellent radar at sorting out junk mail or solicitations. If you use an odd shaped or different colored envelope you'll increase the chance of your mail piece getting opened and looked at.

11. *Make it look "personal".* Use a regular stamp and hand-address the outside envelope if possible. Avoid mailing labels if possible. If you're sending out a fax, jot down a short handwritten message near the top or side of the page.

12. *Focus on ideal prospects only.* With the rising costs of postage and the time involved to put together a successful promotion, you'll be served best by identifying ideal prospects and focusing on them exclusively. You're better of to find a list of say 200 prime prospects versus 2000 potential prospects.

13. *Must have an offer.* Direct marketing is intended to sell a product or service immediately or generate qualified leads for your sales force to follow up with. To make this happen you need an enticing offer to get someone to take action right away.

An offer combines various elements such as the product itself, trial period, the price, guarantee, incentives, terms, and time or quantity limit to name a few. Test, test, test to find out which combination creates the best response to your offer.

14. *Use testimonials and stories.* Third party endorsements are the most powerful form of proof you can use to crack through today's skeptical prospect. Testimonials should be used in every marketing piece you create and use. If you can closely match your testimonials to your target audience the better the results will be.

Weave true stories about your product or service into your offers. We all love stories. Since we were children stories have been used as powerful learning tool. They resonate at the most basic level of our being. Use them to capture the reader and hold your prospect's attention throughout your sales copy.

15. *Use a series of communications.* You've done your homework by identifying key prospects to target. You mail out one direct marketing offer and that's it. This is a big, big mistake that's made by 99% of businesses. You should hit key prospects with multiple offers, mailings and communications. Often times it takes three to seven contacts before someone will take action, place an order, or request more information. Far too many businesses are lazy or won't invest the necessary time to sequence or "farm" out their lists for maximum response and profits.

For example, think about how many times you've gotten something in the mail that you're really interested in, set it on

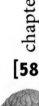

your desk and never responded to it. See what I mean. We've all done it. If you would've received the same or similar offer again a month later, this might have been the reminder you needed to finally take action instead of putting it off or forgetting about it.

KEY CONCEPT: *Employ and utilize the 15 methods listed above to increase response in your direct marketing efforts.* If you're spending money on direct marketing at least give it a fighting chance to hit your target and present a compelling case for your product or service.

MIND CAPTURE LESSON: Direct marketing is often mistakenly thought of as confusing or complex because people don't use the time tested strategies mentioned in this chapter to make their marketing pieces stand out. Far too many businesses put little thought, effort or proven response methods into it and then complain because of little or no response.

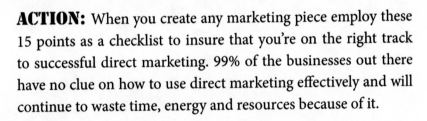

ACTION: When you create any marketing piece employ these 15 points as a checklist to insure that you're on the right track to successful direct marketing. 99% of the businesses out there have no clue on how to use direct marketing effectively and will continue to waste time, energy and resources because of it.

Additional Mind Capture Resources:

Free Report: *"350 of The Best Headlines Ever Written"* send and email to tony@mindcapturegroup.com with the subject line: **350 Report**

Book: *The Ultimate Sales Letter* by Dan Kennedy

Book: *How to Make Your Advertising Make Money* by John Caples

Book: *Making Money With Classified Ads* by Melvin Powers

Book: *Triggers* by Joseph Sugarman

[chapter 11]

THE POWER OF SPIN: HOW TO GET FREE PUBLICITY

The media can make you a fortune if you can master the ability to write a powerful press release. With the massive growth in TV, radio, newspaper and the Internet, there are thousands of opportunities to get free exposure for your business without having to spend more than a little time and a few pennies to send out a fax.

Why should you be using press releases? The answer is simple. They provide you the opportunity to build credibility, gain exposure and generate tons of leads if you know how to hook a writer or producer with a compelling story line or idea. In addition, they have the highest dollar rate of return for any type of marketing if your release gets picked up and your business is featured.

THE 10 BENEFITS OF USING PRESS RELEASES TO MARKET YOUR BUSINESS

1. Low cost. For about 5 to 6 cents you can fax a press release to a potential contact that could pick up your release and print it or use it as feature story.

2. Builds awareness. If people are reading about your business, this is building exposure and awareness for your company.

3. Great way to make announcements or launch new products and promotions. It's a lot easier and cost effective to send out well-written press releases to get attention versus running expensive ads. The media is always on the lookout for something new and exciting to share with their audience.

4. Easy to produce and distribute. Make up a list as you go of targeted media outlets that can be used every time you create and send out a new press release. In addition, the Internet makes it easier than ever to find out whom to contact and their direct phone and fax numbers.

5. The release may turn into a feature article for your business. The quickest way to generate credibility is when your company is selected to be interviewed and featured in a newspaper or magazine. Not only is the story sure to generate new business but it also creates a new and highly effective marketing piece that can be used in future marketing efforts.

6. A lot cheaper than paying for advertising. A full page write up in the local section of your area business section could cost you thousands of dollars if you had to pay for it using advertisements. A small investment of time spent to writing a press release could produce a very profitable return if a story or write up comes from it.

7. Believability factor. People are much more inclined to believe what they see or read about your company in the newspaper versus an ad you've paid for. This may sound strange, but it's a point most people miss. An ad tries to sell you, where a feature story is intended to educate and share with you new, timely and helpful information.

8. Your competitors probably aren't using them to promote themselves. Most people think press releases are difficult to create or they underestimate the power that the media can unleash to help their business. Most small and mid-sized businesses think they have to hire a big PR firm to write, send out and get them published. This is false and untrue.

9. *Piggyback opportunities.* If you've had a favorable story written due to a submitted press release, it's easy to get other media outlets to pick up on it and want to feature your business again for their readership.

10. *They need to fill up space 365 days a year with new, fresh and exciting stories for their audiences.* With the advent of CNN and 24 hour news programming, the media must continue to find new and interesting things to write about or feature. In essence, they need good press releases to make them aware of potential story opportunities.

5 WAYS TO MAKE YOUR PRESS RELEASE STAND OUT AND GET NOTICED

1. *Be controversial.* The media loves controversial people and stories. It may seem like sensationalism, but remember they're in the business to make money and get people stirred up. If you want to quickly get noticed, take a controversial angle with your press releases and trust me - your telephone will start ringing. Be prepared to back up your claims because you'll run across several writers who'll try to discredit your viewpoint and opinions.

2. *Solve a problem.* People are always in search of new information that can help improve their lives. If your product or service can help people save time, money or solve a common problem - that's an excellent foundation for a press release. If the release targets a large percentage of the readership, you dramatically increase the attention your potential story has in a writer's eyes.

3. *Come up with something unique.* What makes you or your company different or unique than everybody else? If you can answer this clearly and hammer it home with a good hook or angle

the power of spin: how to get free publicity

within your press release, you should be able to generate interest. You must always remember that a reporter is continually asking; *"would our readership or viewership benefit and enjoy finding out more about this particular business, person, event, product or service?"*

4. *Make outrageous claims.* If you can create a "buzz" in your release you will attract two types of audiences in the media world: 1. Supporters and 2. Writers who will oppose your viewpoint or stance. The point here is to use a form of "shock value" to get noticed right away. Make sure that if you use this method to make your press release stand out, you'd better be able to back up your claims or else suffer a slew of negative articles and write-ups.

5. *Position your release for mass appeal and interest.* If your release is interesting and targets a large percentage of a particular media's audience, you increase the interest level from the writer at the other end.

5 SIMPLE, YET OFTEN OVERLOOKED MISTAKES MADE WITH PRESS RELEASE YOU SHOULD AVOID

1. *Blatant sales pitch.* If your release is overtly a sales letter in disguise, it will hit the trash can immediately.

2. *Spelling and grammar errors.* Nothing aggravates and sends a negative first impression to a writer quicker than a submitted press release loaded with spelling and grammatical errors.

3. *Don't use the five "W" method.* The basic structure of a press release should always include who, what, when, where and why.

4. *Use only one way to promote the release.* Employ faxes, email, mail and follow-up telephone calls or a combination of these methods to get your release to the media. Some prefer a simple fax, others email and some require a follow up phone call to spark possible interest in what you submitted to them.

5. Poor headline. If you can't capture their attention with a compelling headline, you immediately hurt your chances of success. Remember you're up against several hundred, if not thousands of press releases competing for the media's attention. If you can't hook them in quickly and arouse interest with a strong headline the next release in their stack probably will.

Hopefully I've compelled you enough to use press releases in your marketing arsenal - now let's talk about important tips for creating and using press releases.

Make sure the release has a powerful headline to capture attention. If you can't hook a writer/reporter in the first 3-5 seconds with a good headline, your press release is going directly in the wastebasket. You're often times up against hundreds and thousands of releases each week so you must have a killer headline to hook them in.

Always ask yourself when writing a press release: "who cares?" I learned this from fellow publicity expert Paul Hartunian. He suggests that you ask this question when writing a release to determine if it will have wide enough appeal and interest for a potential newspaper, magazine or talk show to follow up on or possibly feature. If you can't answer this question effectively you dramatically lower your chances of success.

Make the release reader friendly and one page if possible. Double space between sentences and keep it exciting, easy to read and to the point. The goal is to generate interest from the release to generate a follow up phone call or interview from the writer.

Use the five "W" method when creating press releases: Who, what, when, where and why. This is the basic architecture that you should use for every press release.

Make sure there are no spelling errors in the release. Often times if your release is selected the publication will print it word for word as it was submitted. If there are spelling or grammatical errors, the release will 99 times out of 100 end up in the trash.

the power of spin: how to get free publicity

*Include contact information on the top including a name and reliable phone number where you can be reached if a reporter has more questions. If a stressed out, deadline driven reporter can't get to you right away, there's a good chance you'll miss out on free publicity. They have a large stack of other press releases to reference, and they'll move onto the next one if you're tough to reach.

*Realize that your press release may or may not get published even if it is well written and timely. There are no guarantees that a press release will get printed. It's more of an art than a science. If you follow the advice in this chapter you will greatly increase your odds of success.

The next few pages contain press releases I created that pulled amazingly well, and a small sampling of comments I've received from many who've attended my seminars and used my advice. Study these releases and identify things you can use and model for your product, service or organization when crafting press releases.

The first release had an amazing 50% response rate due to the timeliness, angle and fun we had picking on the NFL's Detroit Lions. Media ranging from the Fox News Network to the Detroit Free Press called and did thousands of dollars worth of free PR articles and radio/TV interviews for the website we created.

News Release

FOR IMMEDIATE RELEASE CONTACT: Tony Rubleski (2-pages) 616-638-xxxx

NEW WEBSITE www.recoveringlionsfan.com OFFERS DETROIT LION FOOTBALL FANS ONLINE FORUM TO

ROAR WITH LAUGHTER AND PICK UP UNIQUE GAG GIFTS JUST IN TIME FOR THE HOLIDAY SEASON.

SPRING LAKE, MI – Lions fans unite! A newly created website, *www.recoveringlionsfan.com* will help cheer up your football season blues. The site offers Lions fans, past and present, an outlet to comment, mourn, offer advice, critique and truly laugh with other fans worldwide about the past and present state of Lions' professional football.

Frustrated Detroit Lions fan Tony Rubleski and his brother Jeff came up with the website idea over a cup of coffee while discussing sports. "We were both telling jokes and laughing about how difficult it is to root for Detroit each week but yet we still do," stated Tony Rubleski. Then it hit us both, "Why not create a website to help other disenchanted Lions fans worldwide?" On that fateful day recoveringlionsfan.com was born.

The site offers a wide range of comedic themes ranging from draft pick blunders to humorous interactive sections such as "Where's Barry?" and "12 Step Program" which offers free advice and counseling. In addition, the site also features four unique gag gifts:

1. 2001-2002 RECOVERINGLIONSFAN.COM T-shirt ($10.00 + $3.00 S&H)

2. Package of Five "Game Day" wearable brown bags ($7.00 + $2.00 S&H)

3. Lions 2001-2002 playbook ($7.00 + $2.00 S&H)

4. Celebration "Break In Case of Victory" bag ($10.00 + $2.00 S&H) or Holiday gift package with all four items for $27.95 + $3.50 S&H

Just in time for the holidays, these are sure to get a laugh out of any pro football fan.

"I'm not going to quite my full-time day job to run the site. This is purely therapeutic. If we recoup our costs for design, trademarks, and initial products that would be a bonus.

the power of spin: how to get free publicity

It's been a lot of fun creating the site and initial feedback on the site and products has been amazing. If we can make people smile and see the timely humor of the franchises past 40 years and this seasons 1-12 start it will all be worth it," he laughs.

For more information or interviews contact Tony Rubleski at 616-638-xxxx.

MOLD

750 WAVERLY COURT
HOLLAND, MICHIGAN 49423
(616) 392-▮▮▮▮ • Fax (616) 392-▮▮▮▮

May 11, 2005

Attention: Tony Rubleski
Mind Capture Group
14864 Birchwood Dr.
Spring Lake, Mi. 49456

Dear Mr. Rubleski,

Please accept this letter of testimony as the highest praise LS Mold Inc. can bestow upon you. As Sales and Marketing Manager in one of the toughest business environments I have operated in, was encouraged to participate in your seminar by our management team.

Immediately, I was mentally stimulated and the creative thought processes were engaged. I listened with great interest, and by the end of the seminar I had devised a plan for a press release with the largest impact possible for LS Mold as well as a new customer using your tips as a guideline.

I highly recommend this seminar to any one that is charged with sales and marketing tasks. I learned new techniques to enhance the writing of and increasing the odds of getting press releases printed. In this case due to the nature of the release, great interest in the story has been picked up by two media outlets and I expect this story to take on a life of it's own.

Please use my name as a testimonial and reference as you deem appropriate.

Sincerely,

John T. Bauer
Sales/Marketing Manager
LS Mold Inc.

⚘ Holland Area
⚘ Chamber of Commerce

March 8, 2005

Mind Capture Group
Attn: Tony Rubleski
14864 Birchwood Drive
Spring Lake, MI   49456

Dear Tony,

I wanted to drop you a quick note to thank you for the dynamic and thought provoking program you presented to our members on February 17th! We had an excellent turnout and many positive comments from those in attendance.

Your strategies on how to successfully generate free publicity and deal with the media were invaluable. In particular, the importance of a well written headline in press releases and how to get into the mind of a reporter were two points that really left an impression.

We found your presentation to be polished, fun and professional. We would be pleased to recommend your workshops to other chambers and business associations.

Sincerely,

Jane Clark

Jane Clark, President
Holland Area Chamber of Commerce

[69]

the power of spin: how to get free publicity

KEY CONCEPT: *Use press releases in your marketing mix.*
If you practice this skill it can generate thousands of dollars in

free exposure, build credibility for your company, and attract new business.

MIND CAPTURE LESSON: *The media is everywhere and continually on the lookout for fresh and exciting new stories.* By employing press releases in your marketing arsenal you'll have a hidden advantage over many of your competitors who don't use them or understand how to effectively write them.

ACTION: *Utilize the strategies just outlined and get started.* You should have several things in your business that warrant a press release. If you're stumped take a look at the press release on the next page as a model to review and give you suggestions.

Additional Mind Capture Resources:

DVD: "*How To Get $100,000 In Free Publicity*" *($39 Value)* – click on www.mindcapturegroup.com Mention this page number when you sign up for my free e-letter and you'll receive a special password good toward a free download

Jolene Aubel at Mountain Marketing & Communications 435-649-2183

Book: *6 Steps to Free Publicity* by Marcia Yudkin

Book: *101 Ways to Promote Yourself* by Raleigh Pinskey

Paul Hartunian at www.paulhartunian.com

[chapter 12]
WHERE'S YOUR EVIDENCE?

This scenario happens thousands of times each business day. A company puts new business out for bid, and like clockwork everybody and their brother submits a proposal or goes before the bid committee. Here's the question: How do you stand out from the others and clearly demonstrate why they should choose your firm versus everybody else?

It comes down to one key thing — EVIDENCE!

In an age where customers are deluged with more choices than ever, you need to have strong marketing materials or "evidence" to build credibility with skeptical prospects and win more business. The old clichés such as "great service, lowest prices, highest quality" are overused and simply not believed.

You have to prove your case with strong marketing evidence to win more business. Here are **8 Ways to Strengthen and Build Evidence Into Your Marketing Efforts:**

1.) Use testimonials

2.) Before and after examples

3.) Pictures

4.) Articles about your company

5.) Create and use a company newsletter

6.) Create client lists

7.) Use a powerful guarantee

8.) Reasons why sheet

1. Use testimonials. This one drives me insane because so many businesses don't use them. In my opinion, they are the single most powerful tool you can employ to build credibility, back up your claims, and break down barriers with skeptical prospects. They're 1000 times more believable than any other marketing piece you use to promote yourself.

Testimonials help bridge the gap between skeptical prospects and your marketing message. Use them in all of your marketing!

2. Before and after examples. Give concrete examples or true stories of challenges a client had before doing business with you and how you solved them. This is a powerful way to clearly demonstrate to someone the old adage "if they can do it, so can I".

The entire infomercial (paid programming) industry is built around having great before and after examples to prove their case and drive people to pick up the phone and place an order - often times on pure impulse. Now that's powerful.

3. Pictures. Show off happy customers who use your product or service. Pictures help build interest and reinforce what you or your customers have to say about your company.

A picture is worth a thousand words.

4. Articles about your company. Use favorable newspaper or trade articles about your business or industry to build third-party credibility and interest. People love a good or interesting story. In addition, people have a tendency to believe that your company is legitimate if a newspaper or business publication features you.

5. *Create and use a company newsletter/eletter.* A newsletter has so many excellent benefits that I'm baffled why more businesses don't use them. A good, consistently mailed (at least once a quarter, preferably every month) newsletter adds immense value to your customers and allows you the chance to stay in front of them, entertain, inform, offer new products/services, build goodwill and demonstrate your company's expertise.

If those aren't enough reasons to be using newsletters to market your business, please close this book! That's right – close the book and call me for a full refund. Marketing therapy will not work for you.

6. *Create client lists.* Use a bullet page of major accounts you serve to add validity and recognition when trying to earn new business. If you can create segmented lists by specific industry's (ex. – banks) that's even better. The whole point is to show a prospect that you're reliable and have a history of success.

7. *Use a powerful guarantee.* Back up your claims and offers with such a powerful guarantee that it makes it a no-brainer to do business with you. For example, in our company, we offer a 100% unconditional 1-year guarantee on any marketing tools that we offer at workshops, in our company newsletter, or through one-on-one consulting. This lets our customers and prospects know that we're serious and passionate about our services being able to help their business.

8. *Reasons why sheet.* Create a one-page sheet that lists "5, 7, 10...Reasons To Do Business With Our Company". Take your best benefits and solutions and condense them into simple,

where's your evidence

concise bullet points that clearly demonstrate the advantages of doing business with you.

If you have problems coming up with more than a few benefits, call or survey your existing customers and ask them point blank "why do you use our company? You'll be amazed at the excellent feedback you'll get to add to your marketing arsenal.

Remember to use "Evidence" in **ALL** of your marketing efforts to win new business and increase your company's bottom line.

├────────────────┤

KEY CONCEPT: *Always be thinking about ways you can PROVE your expertise in today's complex and skeptical marketplace.* People are deluged with too many choices, make it easy for them to pick you.

MIND CAPTURE LESSON: The more you use strong marketing evidence in the marketplace, the more business you'll get. Plain and simple, people are looking for honesty and competence in a world increasingly in short supply of it!

ACTION: Review all of your current marketing and advertising programs to identify where you're currently using the eight methods of evidence we discussed in this chapter. Work on incorporating each of these strategies into your marketing efforts to achieve better positioning, credibility and results.

Additional Mind Capture Resources:
Book: *Clicking* by Faith Popcorn
Book: *Influence* by Robert Cialdini
Book: *MindControlMarketing.com* by Mark Joyner

[chapter 13]

NICHES-TO-RICHES
THE POWER OF VERTICAL MARKETING

Picture the perfect customer in your mind. What do they look like? What do they like about your product or service? Can you turn them into a source of vertical marketing excellence and wealth?

These are a few questions you should be asking if you want to grow your business with fewer headaches. Identifying prime vertical markets help businesses do three key things:

1.) Save a huge amount of time and frustration in your sales and marketing efforts

2.) Increases sales, retention levels and the amount of highly qualified referrals

3.) Positions you as a valuable and credible company to do business with

Let's look at each of these three areas to determine how you can quickly identify vertical markets for your business.

Save time and frustration with your sales and marketing. Marketing is a learned skill. You either work at it or risk being left behind. Far too many businesses take whatever business they can get without any thought as to where it came from and if it's worth their time or resources. "They walk over dollars to pick up dimes" is the best analogy for this type of marketing sin.

Finding highly qualified niches that tightly match your product or service offerings takes a lot of the guesswork and waste out of your marketing. An expert marksman always uses a precision rifle to hit the bull's eye - not a shotgun. This is unfortunately what far too many businesses do. They use mass marketing versus intense, consistent and focused marketing only to key prospects that have the highest chance or probability of doing business with them.

A consistent follow up attack to a highly qualified list of prospects is far superior than mass marketing. Unless you're a huge company with millions of dollars to burn, vertical marketing is the most efficient and effective way to generate leads and new business for any business.

Increases sales, retention levels and the amount of highly qualified referrals. The huge benefit to vertical markets is that you dramatically increase your chances of getting new business because you become known in that industry or niche as the "expert".

For example, I work with a lot of insurance agents. One of my key training clients is a regional based company that competes against many larger national insurance firms. I'm so in tune with what they're looking for that I've had several of them tell me I think like them and would make a great representative for the company. Where did they draw that conclusion? It's easy: I speak their language, understand their marketing challenges and have a clear grasp of how to help them. With that in mind; when

I meet with a new agent I'm positioned as someone that knows their business needs - which translates into them trusting me and our company earning their business.

With intense competition and more choices in today's market, maintaining and keeping customers is becoming extremely challenging. By positioning yourself in a few key industries, your relationships and specific industry knowledge make it much harder for a new competitor to come in and wrestle away the business from you.

If you've done effective follow-up as we've suggested throughout the book, you'll be light years ahead of your competition. They'll have a hell of a time breaking the lock off the vault to even meet with your customers, yet alone win their trust and business.

As your reputation begins to grow in an industry, you'll begin to receive much better referrals based on your track record and industry client lists. We see this in our business quite often. We work with many regional chains of gas stations in the Midwest and we find that when we receive a referral into a prospective account, we simply list off all the other chains we currently serve. This builds instant credibility and makes the sales process much easier.

Positions you as a valuable and credible company to do business with. By becoming an expert in a niche, you increase the value of your services because your company is no longer viewed as just another vendor that can be replaced via a competitive bid or a fancy sales presentation from a rival firm.

In the age of information overload people are often too busy or burned out with all the different options available to them, that they seek out firms with solid reputations to save time and to increase the odds of making a good buying decision. In tightly linked vertical markets, your customers and prospects can either build your business or quickly blacklist you if your product or

niches to riches

service isn't up to par. If you can deliver on your promises, the positive word of mouth will make your job that much easier.

Niche and Be Rich!

—————————|————————|

KEY CONCEPT: *Identifying key niches that benefit from your product or services is key to your success.* Targeting specific niches helps increase the odds in your favor by generating better referrals, and positions your company as an expert in that industry. In addition, it maximizes and leverages your time and marketing dollars.

MIND CAPTURE LESSON: Look for ways to be a big fish in a small pond by targeting vertical markets that respond best to your offers. The old adage *"jack-of-all trades, master of none"* is the biggest mistake businesses make when looking for new business.

ACTION: Examine your customer list and determine which groups and vertical markets respond best to your offers. Make sure you intensely focus and allocate your marketing dollars to target similar prospects that have the highest probability of working with you.

MIND CAPTURE LOYALTY

[chapter 14]
THE LIST IS YOUR MOST VALUED BUSINESS POSSESSION

Three crimes are committed millions of times day after day by most businesses, and sales professionals that not only robs their customers but also drastically hurts their chance for long-term success. What are the three you ask?

#1: Not collecting pertinent customer and prospect data

#2: Little if any consistent communication to existing and prospective customers

#3: Not making enough offers

Top direct mail and catalog companies can teach us all a valuable lesson as to why capturing customer and prospect information is their #1 business asset. They know the massive value and leverage an accurate, and detailed customer/prospect list gives them when creating new marketing and sales offers to drive revenues and repeat business.

I want you to imagine someone playing the dangerous game of Russian roulette. With each pull of the hammer, they'll either live or if they hit the wrong chamber it's all over. The odds are one in six. Now obviously being in business is not life threatening and you're not playing with bullets, but it ranks right up there with how incredibly risky it is to not capture customer names

Now folks, this is common sense but let me share with you how common this problem is. Time after time I look through a businesses database and cringe in horror at what I discover. Everything from outdated addresses, missing data, no purchase history to such vital and unforgivable things as proper contact names, email addresses and names of key customers or contacts.

By far the two biggest offenders when it comes to not capturing customer information are restaurants and small retail shops. They let a fortune walk in and out of their locations day after day with little if any plan to capture data on who these people are and what they purchased. When things slow down they're left with the choice of praying or "hoping" for people to stop in or running costly and often ill-timed advertising blitzes to possibly generate in-store traffic and business. This equates to gambling where sadly the house or media rep often wins more times than the retailer who's counting on a marketing 21 or throwing a seven with the advertising dice.

A second major crime is lack of communication to existing and prospective customers. Here's a startling statistic you should plaster in your planner, computer and office wall as a powerful visual reminder to the importance of staying in frequent contact:

For Each Month That Goes By Without Some Form of Communication To Existing Customers, An Average of 10% Top of Mind Awareness Goes Out The Door

When I ask audiences how many of them communicate at least once a month through direct mail, email, fax, or in-person, with their customers a typical response is less than 20%. This is baffling and disturbing at the same time. The quickest way to combat retention issues and spend valuable marketing dollars is to establish a strategic and consistent contact plan with customers and key prospects.

The Power of A Defined, Planned Out Yearly Promotion and
Contact Calendar for Key Prospects & Current Customers

People have hundreds of options and competing offers thrown at them daily that the odds increase greatly for them to defect or spend their money somewhere else simply because they forget about you and someone else appears at exactly the moment when a new or additional need arises.

This is where having a 12-month marketing schedule mapped out and in motion is so valuable. Simply lay out by month an action plan for two sets of defined groups: 1. Existing customers and 2. Key prospects. Keep the plan in motion and resist the temptation at all costs to skip a month or deviate from the plan you originally created.

For example, here's how a bank could map out a 12-month marketing or contact plan for existing corporate banking accounts:

JANUARY: New Year's service review/visit with top commercial accounts

FEBRUARY: Valentine's Day related "We Love Your Business" mailing/offer

MARCH: First quarter newsletter containing new offers and promotions

APRIL: Spring "Referral Rewards" contest

MAY: Client appreciation event and educational seminar

JUNE: Second quarter newsletter containing updates and promotions

JULY: Fourth of July "Movie Madness" promo – send key accounts 10 free movie passes to give to their employees and family members

AUGUST: Summer customer survey via mail, email, phone and in-person

SEPTEMBER: Third quarter newsletter

OCTOBER: Roll out new promo and "Summer Survey" results and feedback

the list is your most valued business possession

NOVEMBER: Thanksgiving card and "thank you" Holiday luncheon

DECEMBER: Fourth quarter newsletter

The third major crime is not presenting enough offers to existing and prospective customers.

What's The Best Way To Test & Roll Out A New Product or Service?

Introduce it to your best current customers. This seems blazingly obvious but the folly I continue to see within lots of company's, all shapes and sizes, tells me otherwise. Why do you test to existing customers first? Easy. These folks have already demonstrated they trust you and are willing to consider and respond to additional "new" promotions and offers.

An even easier way to gauge if a new product or service is worth offering is to survey 20 of your top customers. Simply call them, email or ask them face-to-face to give you honest feedback on a possible new item you're thinking of adding into your business and if it's something they'd be interested in. If you receive a large amount of positive feedback and even pre-orders you're on to something. If the reaction is rather luke warm or negative, save yourself time, grief and money and spend little if any time doing a test launch or new product roll out within your customer base.

Forget focus groups, and massive marketing campaigns until you've first tested your newest offering at a smaller and more cost effective level. If the response is good, then proceed with a small rollout to new prospects.

People are always looking for additional products and services from existing suppliers for one central reason: time savings. With the trust and goodwill already established they're very receptive to looking at additional offers that can improve their lives but more importantly save them time. In a busy, and complex market with high levels of skepticism particularly related to advertising, people are very careful about who they choose to do business with.

KEY CONCEPT: *Accurate and updated customer information is the most valuable asset within any business.* Without it the business is severely limited in its ability to communicate with customers and roll out additional product or service offerings.

MIND CAPTURE LESSON: Always be capturing new client data and updating your files. In addition, always stay in front of key customers with updates and new offers to increase sales, loyalty and maintain awareness of your company.

ACTION: Start today to make this a priority within your business and always be on the lookout for ideas, information and new product/service offerings that make sense to introduce and roll out to existing customers.

the list is your most valued business possession

[chapter 15]
CREATING CUSTOMER LOYALTY

Does customer loyalty still exist? In today's challenging economy when you ask business owners this question you'll get a wide range of answers. I firmly believe that customer loyalty is quickly disappearing.

The reasons:

*The Internet and the ability to price shop

*New competitors continually entering the market

*Pathetic service and little if any follow up with existing customers

Before we look at several excellent ways to increase loyalty and diminish the chance of defection from existing customers, let's begin with a quick reality check or **3 "Truths" You Should Know About Your Customers They Don't Teach At Harvard Business School:**

1.) Friendly competition is a HUGE lie! Remember it's called competition and the goal is to win new business. Your competitors are trying to pick off your customers, your livelihood and your money.

2.) If you're not communicating with your customers consistently, START TODAY – the choice is yours! Every month that goes by without some sort of update, offer or communication is very dangerous and the threat of customer defection increases.

3.) Your customers are NOT spending nearly as much with you as they really could or should be! They're going somewhere else to get additional products or services because they either; a. don't know you have it available or b. your competition is picking off dollars you should be getting.

Customer loyalty can never be taken for granted. The only thing a business can do is implement ways to build goodwill through the use of focused and consistent channels of communication in order to help reduce the chance your customer will go elsewhere.

27 Ways to Keep Your Customers Coming Back Again & Again

1. Be fun to do business with. The landscape is littered with mechanical, dull, mundane businesses that have no personality or fun. If you want to stand out from everyone else, make it fun to do business with you. Some examples: Contests, parties, seminars or special sales events for your clients.

2. Recognize special events. For example, when your customer celebrates a birthday, anniversary, wins an award or is featured in the local press, send them a short note, article reprint, or give them a phone call. They'll appreciate you thinking about them.

3. Create and use a company newsletter. This is a biggie. Most businesses use the "we're too busy" excuse when it comes to creating and mailing out a customer newsletter. This is a tragic mistake. Why? You can find a local designer, intern or college student to do this for you. You give them the content and ideas and let them handle the design element. Company newsletters are an excellent way to stay in front of your customers and announce new product or service offerings.

4. *Special mailings or offers.* Use mail, postcards, email, and faxes to stay in contact with customers. Holiday events, "early-bird" discounts, coupons, and special announcements are just a few things you can use.

5. *Have contests or giveaways.* Offer cash, prizes, discounts or special recognition to build repeat business, referrals, and to recognize your biggest customer advocates.

6. *Thank you notes.* Simple, quick, easy and very effective. I know it's too easy to do, but not so easy to actually pull off. I'm amazed at how few businesses even do this.

7. *Offer additional products or services.* YES, your customers want to spend more money with you. If they already trust you they'll be eager to buy more often from you. The #1 mistake people make: They don't offer enough new products or services to their satisfied customers.

8. *Refer them business.* Help them to be successful. If you're patronizing their business or referring prospects to them it shows that you truly understand their business and want to help them.

9. *Return calls within 48 hours.* 24 hours is always best, but often not always possible. Don't delay on questions, problems, etc. – get back to your customers within 1-2 days be it through the phone, email or voicemail.

10. *Have a professional answer your main telephone line.* This one really gets me. Far too many businesses have someone who's either rude, incompetent or poorly trained handling incoming phone calls. This is a huge mistake. Get someone good to handle this critical function.

11. *Offer a strong guarantee.* Back up your claims and stand behind what you sell. For example, I offer a 150% unconditional money back guarantee at all of our seminars. I feel confident in my training and product packages to make such a bold claim.

12. *Under promise – over deliver.* Sounds cliché but few if any businesses pull it off on a consistent basis. Make it a goal to deliver more value, guarantees, quality, and fun than your competition and you'll keep them coming back again and again.

13. *Create and use continuity programs.* Simply put: Hook your customers into spending more money with you by using some sort of additional bonus or discount based on number of visits, dollars spent, or purchases. For example, buy nine shirts, get the tenth one free. Or, spend $100 and receive 10% off, spend $200 and get $15% off, etc.

14. *Preferred customer program.* This is a great way to reward and recognize your top customers by offering them special discounts, offers, freebies or bonuses. Use the 80/20 rule with your top customers to get them to spend more.

15. *Referral program.* Pay cash, give gifts, offer discounts or have contests to entice your customers to give you more referrals. If you're doing a great job and make it worth their while, they'll seek out ways to help you build your business.

16. *Survey your customers.* Why? You'll find out what additional products and services they'd like you to offer, what areas you're strong in, and what areas need improvement.

17. *Mystery shop your competition.* This does three key things: 1. helps you find their strengths and weaknesses 2. great way to pick up new ideas/insights and 3. great way to scout potential talent you may want working for you

18. *Use celebrities.* You'd be amazed at how many well-known sports, TV or political celebs are available to help promote your business at fairly reasonable prices. It could even be someone in your hometown or region that's well known or respected.

19. *Hold seminars and specials events.* Hold special free breakfasts, luncheons or private parties for your best customers. Ask them to bring along a friend or business associate. Be sure to offer good speakers or topics that are either fun or offer relevant and timely information.

20. *Comment cards.* Use these to track who's doing business with you and what they like or would enjoy seeing. The old fishbowl drawing for a FREE item, prize or lunch sounds too simple but it still works quite nicely.

21. *Mail them relevant articles about their company, industry or competitors.* They'll appreciate it and think of you as a resource. In addition, it may be something written up about their company they missed or overlooked.

22. *Educate them.* Send them free reports, books or videos, or offer classes and workshops that will benefit them. People love to learn new things.

23. *Send birthday cards.* You could use it for number of years they've done business with you or for their own personal birthday. We ALL love a little recognition.

24. *Give client awards. Mail or deliver special awards (certificate, plaque, gift) to key customers.*

creating customer loyalty

You could recognize anything ranging from years in business, 50ᵗʰ order placed with your company - to civic events they actively donate time and money to.

25. *Special contests or sales.* Tie in with different promotions or calendar events. Example – "back to school", "boss is out of town", Thanksgiving, etc.

26. *Special "Thank-You" sales events or discounts.* Offer early bird discounts, preferred customer pricing or club member type promotions to encourage membership, repeat business, and recognition with your customers.

27. *Stay in front of them often.* Use a well thought out and precise marketing mix such as newsletters, email, postcards, sales, events, and recognition programs to build loyalty, referrals and your bank account.

If you treat customer retention as a marketing strategy you'll accomplish 3 KEY things in the market place:

1. Solid reputation and higher customer retention

2. Increased sales and growth

3. More referral business

├───────────────────┤

KEY CONCEPT: *Creating Customer Loyalty.* Realize that loyalty is earned and cultivated by bringing value to the market and continually staying in front of your customers.

MIND CAPTURE LESSON: Create and use a follow up system for staying in continual contact with your customers to build repeat purchases, referrals and loyalty.

ACTION: We covered 27 ways to build loyalty with your existing customers. Pick a few that make sense, make them a priority and get them going immediately. If you don't have a solid plan for staying in continual contact with your customers, you substantially increase the odds of losing future sales and referrals. The choice is yours!

Additional Mind Capture Resources:

Book: *Customers For Life* by Carl Sewell

Bob & Susan Negen - www.WhizBangTraining.com

Book: *Customer Satisfaction Is Worthless, Customer Loyalty Is Priceless* by Jeffrey Gitomer

Book: *Sam Walton: Made In America* by Sam Walton

[99]

creating customer loyalty

[chapter 16]
COMPLACENCY = DEATH

Let me throw out a challenging question that I use with companies of all shapes and sizes:

McDonald's is a huge, well-known company that sells millions of burgers each day simply on the strength of its name. Why do they still continue to advertise?

This should elicit a variety of answers in your head. But think about this question more closely. Whether you agree with their ad campaigns or not is irrelevant. The whole point of this question is to make businesses realize that no matter how good things are going, things can change in an instant!

I laugh when talking with companies that have the smug attitude of "we're so successful that we don't need to market or advertise". I've got news for you Mr./Mrs. Business owner:

THE COMPANIES THAT YOU WOULD THINK HAVE IT MADE, STILL CONTINUE TO AGGRESIVELY MARKET, PROMOTE AND ADVERTISE DURING GOOD TIMES AND BAD.

Why? Complacency equals death. It's that simple.

The great Albert Einstein said the definition of insanity is "doing the same thing over and over again and expecting a different result." This amazing scientist could've easily written a book on marketing because he perfectly describes the illness holding back too many businesses, sales professionals and entrepreneurs.

Having critiqued countless marketing pieces and answering hundreds of questions from audiences, eletter subscribers and clients the last few years I can tell you there's a dangerous delusion regarding marketing that cripples and holds many businesses and non-profit organizations hostage.

Read on if you dare...this amazingly simple point can revolutionize your marketing. It's called The Silver Bullet Theory.

Unlike the movies where all it takes is a silver bullet to kill the blood thirsty vampire and everyone in the audience celebrates, growing a business in competitive times isn't that easy. The Silver Bullet Theory:

Foolish belief that one form of media exists to solve
all of your marketing and sales challenges

When the Silver Bullet Theory rears its ugly head and attacks the mind of the would-be marketer it has many dangerous consequences. Instead of planting marketing seeds for future growth and referrals when times were good and the balance sheet was in the black, the business now finds itself in search of a magic solution to the new challenges presenting themselves.

The Power of Using A Marketing Mix To Get An Unfair Advantage Over Your Competition

If you've read this far you'll clearly see that I think business is a game measured in wins AND in losses. If your marketing is producing more wins on a consistent basis than losses you'll probably remain in business. If not, you'll end up in the pile of "broken dreams" joining legions of companies that are no longer around.

By employing a marketing mix to generate a consistent flow of new business and referrals, you'll be ahead of 95% of your competitors. Why? Most people are so busy and end up trapped working in their businesses, that they foolishly treat marketing as a non-priority. They either procrastinate, or worse they put this critically important function in the hands of incompetent people.

Starting today, make it your goal to use a consistent, thought out marketing mix to keep your business growing!

If you plan to pour your heart, soul and time into an enterprise, why not strive to be the best. Keep your competitors guessing as to how they're going to keep up with you.

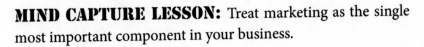

KEY CONCEPT: *Complacency equals death.* Marketing is not to be treated lightly.

MIND CAPTURE LESSON: Treat marketing as the single most important component in your business.

ACTION: Analyze, review and track all of your current and future marketing efforts. Set up and use a marketing mix to stay ahead of the competition.

complacency = death

[chapter 17]

REFERRAL MAGIC:
HOW TO GET MORE

Ilove referrals. Don't you? In this next section I'd like to walk you through the psychology of why we give and get referrals and how to get tons more. The number one reason I love referrals - they are the most qualified kind of lead you can find! Nothing else even comes close. A good, solid referral has an 80 to 90% chance of becoming a new customer if handled properly.

Here are seven powerful reasons we give and receive referrals:

1.) *The feelings of <u>goodwill</u> and gratitude they generate*

2.) *To direct others to a <u>trustworthy</u> and reliable source*

3.) *To show <u>knowledge</u> and credibility*

4.) *For selfishness or <u>personal gain</u>*

5.) *To create <u>new</u> relationships*

6.) *Strengthen existing relationships*

7.) *To help or be helped by others*

WHY YOU SHOULD AGRESSIVELY SEEK OUT REFERRALS EVERYDAY

1. INEXPENSIVE. Compared to any other form of advertising or lead-generation they're a steal in cost.

2. EASIER TO WORK WITH. A good referral is typically qualified and pre-sold on your product or service simply through the third-party recommendation from the person that referred you to them.

3. MUCH HIGHER CLOSE RATIO. A good, solid referral has about an 80-90% chance of becoming a new client if handled properly.

4. EASY TO GET. If you ask – you shall receive. We'll show you a few simple ways to generate a ton of referrals.

5. BUILDS GOODWILL. If you ask for referrals and get them, this clearly demonstrates that your product or service is excellent. When a customer trusts and values your business, getting referrals is a breeze. So many businesses are "afraid" to ask for them. Wake up people. Referrals are powerful reflection on the health of your business.

5 PROVEN WAYS TO GENERATE MORE REFERRALS

1.) Power questions

2.) Direct mail

3.) Contests and promotions

4.) Pass along offer

5.) Reward program

By employing even one or more of these strategies, you'll see a marked improvement in the amount of NEW, high-quality referral business generated for your business!

1. POWER QUESTIONS

The goal is to generate specific referrals from customers and people you meet while networking, based on powerful "referral generating" questions. Here are a few:

"Who do you know that constantly complains about their ___ _____ (staffing, insurance, accountant, etc.)?"

"We work with a lot of _____ (banks, car dealerships, restaurants), do you know of anyone that you do business within this industry that we might be able to help?"

"I'll be contacting other _____ (banks, travel agents, etc.) is there anyone in particular you recommend in (Grand Rapids, Rockford, Muskegon) that might benefit from our services?"

"Who would you recommend I contact within your company regarding _____?" (good for internal referrals within an organization)

BONUS STRATEGY: The following statement is designed to peak a prospects interest in your product or service when they ask the inevitable question, "what do you do?"

"Do you know how businesses _____, we help _____."

Here's what we use: *"Do you know how businesses spend a lot of money on marketing, but often get poor results - we help them eliminate this and generate results!"*

2. DIRECT MAIL

For those who are too timid to ask for referrals or wish there were an easy way to get referrals, you'll love this section. I'm about to share how a simple two-page letter can generate a ton of testimonials and referrals for any business!

WE COULD CHARGE THOUSANDS OF DOLLARS FOR THIS LETTER AND PROBABLY GET IT FOR ONE MAIN REASON: <u>THIS LETTER WORKS</u>!

I call this the MISSION IMPOSSIBLE LETTER. At the end of this section on referrals I've enclosed the actual letter that we've created and use for our business. This simple letter, if slightly modified to fit your business will produce HUGE responses when mailed to your existing customers.

Why does this letter work so effectively?

1.) It creates curiosity

2.) It uses a compelling headline – "grabs" their attention

3.) People can relate to it – most people know about Mission Impossible (TV, or movie)

4.) The letter is simple, direct and to the point

5.) It's an honest letter – we tell them why we're contacting them

6.) It's time friendly

7.) Humorous

8.) Ease of response – they can mail it back in the enclosed SASE or fax it to our office

The letter does three key things: 1. Produces referrals 2. Gets testimonials 3. Keeps your marketing current and provides instant feedback

3. CONTESTS AND PROMOTIONS

Why should you use contests and promotions to generate referrals? It's simple: THEY WORK!!! A good contest or promotion does five key things:

1. *Increases response.* People like to be acknowledged when they refer

2. *Gets people excited.* Everyone loves a good contest.

3. *Fun.* God knows we need to have more fun in our lives.

4. *Easy to put together.* This doesn't have to be a big, complex project.

5. *Great way to reward people for referrals.* Gives them more incentive to help you.

Ideas for contest giveaways:

- Trips

- Money

- Merchandise or services

- "Night-Out" getaways

- Concert or sports tickets

- Movie passes

- Gift certificates

referral magic: how to get more

4. PASS ALONG OFFER

A pass along offer is simply where you ask a customer or another business to pass along a special offer, discount, free-trial offer or other information about your product or service to someone they know.

How do you get a pass along offer to existing clients and prospects?

- Mail it to them

- Include it in your billing statements

- Put it in your company newsletter or enewsletter

- Insert the offer into their bag (retail approach) when they make a purchase

- Give it to them directly

- Do joint ventures with other businesses that see the value of your product or service

An excellent example of a company that uses pass along offers well is Omaha Steaks. Stop and really think about what they do for a minute. They sell steaks through the mail! If they can pull this off and use a very effective pass along offer on their return envelopes, then anyone can do this. I don't care if you sell widgets or software, this can be employed by any business.

If you haven't seen their direct mail and the pass along offer they use – shame on you. You'll have to call them and request information. They are EXCELLENT marketers and you should study anything and everything they do.

5. REWARD PROGRAM

I'm a firm believer in rewarding and recognizing people when they refer prospects or new business to our company. Here's the magic question you should always be asking when you get a referral: **"How did you hear about us?"**

If you can't track where you're getting referrals from you face two major challenges,

1.) You can't thank or reward the person who made the referral to you

2.) You have no way of encouraging them to give you more

By simply asking - "how did you hear about us?" you can rid yourself of this problem.

HERE ARE 7 EXCELLENT AND AFFORDABLE "REFERRAL RE-WARD" IDEAS THAT ANY BUSINESS CAN USE:

1. *Gift certificates* – we all like to shop especially when it's free

2. *Books* – books on business, success, or a persons favorite hobbies are always well received

3. *Movie passes* – everyone likes to go to the movies

4. *Magazine subscription* – every month they'll be thinking of you when their favorite magazine arrives at home or the office

5. *Discounts* – offer a coupon or discount on future products or services

6. *Lotto tickets* – simple, inexpensive and a fun way to thank and maybe even put a little money in their pocket

7. *Candy* – Everyone has a sweet tooth

REMEMBER: A thank you gift/reward should always be genuine and not intended as a bribe for future favors or help.

KEY CONCEPT: *Seek out more referrals. They are the best kind of lead you can get.*

MIND CAPTURE LESSON: Referral opportunities are everywhere if you focus on using the right questions and methods. Use some of the strategies from this chapter to get more.

ACTION: We listed five proven ways to get more referrals and ways to reward people when you get them. These methods work. Get busy and start using them in your business!

Additional Mind Capture Resources:
Book: *Endless Referrals* by Bob Burg
Book: *The Sales Bible* by Jeffrey Gitomer
Book: *How to Sell Anything To Anybody* by Joe Girard

———————————

The next few pages show two versions of the Mission Impossible letter that can be modified and used for your particular product/service.

"MISSION IMPOSSIBLE"
3-27-06
Valued Mind Capture Group Client:

Your mission should you choose to accept it: **Write down or type up a few comments** about your experience with Mind Capture Group and the training or consulting services you've utilized to help your business. This could range from the positive impact we've had on your sales, marketing programs, repeat and referral business, positive publicity or other benefits directly linked to positive results to your company's bottom line. *The lines below are open for your comments:*

_____

_____

_____

_____

Name: _____

Company: _____

OK – Why do you want my comments?

Simple. We're conducting a new marketing campaign this spring to identify other businesses that can benefit from our dynamic marketing, referral and publicity training programs. Your comments will be of great help when meeting with new prospects and referrals who'd like to learn more about how we can be of service.

We know you're busy so we have a special FREE gift set aside for you **As our way of saying <u>THANK</u> <u>YOU</u> for taking a minute to help out!**

You have tons of things already piled up on your desk and we'd like to reward you for taking a minute to respond. The "special" thank- you could be movie passes or dinner/merchant gift certificates. One lucky WINNER will receive a FREE training session!

WARNING:
This page WILL self-destruct in 5 minutes unless it's filled in and returned ☺

referral magic: how to get more

(Continued on next page…)

Please return your comments in the enclosed S.A.S.E. or fax them back to 616-.... If you have additional questions please give me a call at 616....

Your Partner In Success!

Tony Rubleski
President – Mind Capture Group, LLC

PS: If you know of one or two other companies or trusted business associates that can benefit from our dynamic training programs, please fill in the section below and either return it with your comments in the S.A.S.E. or fax them to our office.

Tony, please contact the following people who'd like to learn how Mind Capture Group can help their business:

1. Name: _____
   Company: _____
   Phone/email: _____

2. Name: _____
   Company: _____
   Phone/email: _____

THANK YOU for your Referrals. Your confidence in us is truly appreciated and never taken for granted!

(Please insert into SASE or fax filled in pages to 616...)

[chapter 18]

10 SERIOUS MARKETING QUESTIONS YOU SHOULD ALWAYS BE ASKING

1.) What marketing mix will we employ to build Mind Capture?

2.) **What are the timelines for implementation of each component in the mix?** This is key because most people won't implement change unless it's treated as a priority and given a firm deadline for completion.

3.) Who are our top three vertical markets or industries that have the highest profit margin and need for our product or service?

4.) Where do we visualize our business to be one, three, five and ten years down the road and how will we get it there?

5.) What forms of marketing "evidence" will we use in our marketing efforts to build credibility and generate more sales?

6.) How do we leverage our existing business to generate more referral business from satisfied customers?

7.) What creative ways and systems will we use to continually stay in contact with customers and prospects?

8.) How will we use the media to build and promote our business?

9.) **What's our plan for future training and learning** (seminars, books, networking, etc.)**?**

10.) How will we improve our current marketing to incorporate proven direct marketing strategies to make it more effective?

[additional MIND CAPTURE resources]

*Dale Carnegie, *How to Win Friends and Influence People*
*Thomas Friedman, *The World Is Flat*
*Robert Allen & Mark Victor Hansen, *The One
        Minute Millionaire*
*Sam Walton, *Made In America: My Story*
*Napoleon Hill, *Think & Grow Rich*
*Robert Ringer, *Winning Through Intimidation*
*Maxwell Maltz, *The New Psycho-Cybernetics*
*Greg Bauer, *The Breathing Blanket*
*Shelly Brady, *The Ten Things I Learned from Bill Porter*
*John Caples, *How to Make Your Advertising Make Money*
*Joseph Cossman, *How I Made $1,000,000 in Mail Order*
*Donald Trump, *Surviving At The Top*
*Seth Godin, *Permission Marketing*
*Jon Spoelstra, *Marketing Outrageously*
*Og Mandino, *The Greatest Salesman in the World*
*Jose Silva, *Sales Power – The Silva Mind Method*
*Zig Ziglar, *Ziglar On Selling*
*Richard Marcinko, *Secrets of the Rogue Warrior*
*Thomas Friedman, *The Lexus and The Olive Tree*
*Thomas Stanley & William Danko, *The Millionaire
        Next Door*

*Dexter Yeager, *The Pursuit*
*Mark Victor Hansen & Jack Canfield, *The Aladdin Factor*
*Andy Andrews, *The Traveler's Gift*
*T. Harv Eker, *Secrets of the Millionaire Mind*
*James Allen, *As A Man Thinketh*
*Joe Vitale & Jo Han Mok, *The E-Code*

NEW WEBSITE www.recoveringlionsfan.com OFFERS DETROIT LION FOOTBALL FANS ON-LINE FORUM TO ROAR WITH LAUGHTER AND PICK UP UNIQUE GAG GIFTS JUST IN TIME FOR THE HOLIDAY SEASON.

SPRING LAKE, MI – Lions fans unite! A newly created website, *www.recoveringlionsfan.com* will help cheer up your football season blues. The site offers Lions fans, past and present, an outlet to comment, mourn, offer advice, critique and truly laugh with other fans worldwide about the past and present state of Lions' professional football.

Frustrated Detroit Lions fan Tony Rubleski and his brother Jeff came up with the website idea over a cup of coffee while discussing sports. "We were both telling jokes and laughing about how difficult it is to root for Detroit each week but yet we still do," stated Tony Rubleski. Then it hit us both, "Why not create a website to help other disenchanted Lions fans worldwide?" On that fateful day recoveringlionsfan.com was born.

The site offers a wide range of comedic themes ranging from draft pick blunders to humorous interactive sections such as "Where's Barry?" and "12 Step Program" which offers free advice and counseling. In addition, the site also features four unique gag gifts:

1. 2001-2002 RECOVERINGLIONSFAN.COM T-shirt ($10.00 + $3.00 S&H)

2. Package of Five "Game Day" wearable brown bags ($7.00 + $2.00 S&H)

3. Lions 2001-2002 playbook ($7.00 + $2.00 S&H)

4. Celebration "Break In Case of Victory" bag ($10.00 + $2.00 S&H) or Holiday gift package with all four items for $27.95 + $3.50 S&H

Just in time for the holidays, these are sure to get a laugh out of any pro football fan.

"I'm not going to quite my full-time day job to run the site. This is purely therapeutic. If we recoup our costs for design, trademarks, and initial products that would be a bonus.

It's been a lot of fun creating the site and initial feedback on the site and products has been amazing. If we can make people smile and see the timely humor of the franchises past 40 years and this seasons 1-12 start it will all be worth it," he laughs.

For more information or interviews contact Tony Rubleski at 616-638-xxxx.

Printed in the United States
55491LVS00004B/175-1509